GW01605769

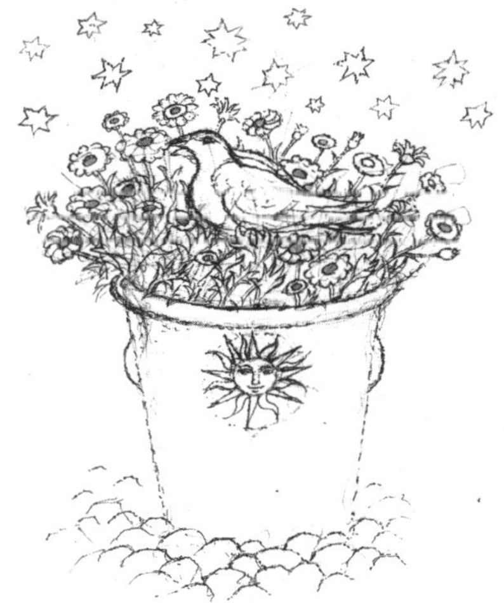

In memory of my parents, whose support and encouragement is not forgotten.

# LIFELINES

## Selected drawings of Truda Lane

*to dearest Elizabeth*
*with love from Truda*

# FOREWORD by John Moat

There have always been artists – and most often, it seems, they are women – who from the outset bring to their work a vision so innately their own, so realised, and so much a part of their own distinctive way of expression, that we tend to view them as apart from their time, impossible to categorise, and so perhaps eccentric. They come with an integrity complete, and perhaps with that quality W B Yeats called "unity of being" which affords their work a self-expressive immediacy, authentic, original and free from any obvious influence. For instance, among poets, Emily Dickenson, Stevie Smith; among novelists, Jean Rhys, Ivy Compton-Burnett; among painters, Gwen John, Winifred Nicholson, Mary Newcomb. This same quality, as always the more conclusive for being entirely unselfconscious, is the hallmark of Truda Lane's work.

It's unusual for a serious artist to have devoted so much of her life to what one might have supposed was the limiting means of drawing. Early on there were paintings, but at the Slade already Truda was beginning to bring her focus to draughtsmanship – for which as a student she was awarded prizes. Shortly after, she and her husband, John Lane, painter and writer, went to live in Yorkshire. "I lost my heart to that glorious North Riding landscape in a way I've not done since. And

*Front cover* **Wolfish dog in a winter landscape**
As snow fell, a large wild-looking dog transformed an everyday landscape into something remarkable.
brush/watercolour 38 x 57 cm
*Back cover* **Barnstaple rooftop**
watercolour 15 x 22.5 cm
*Page 1* **Dove roosting among daisies**
indian ink & watercolour 13 x 15 cm

through that wild landscape I have sought expression for human emotion and life's struggles."

In these early drawings her idiom – the series of searching lines that somehow discover an extraordinary strength, her simple but highly tensile compositions, economy of wash and hints of colour that seem to spring naturally from the drawing itself, even the occasional startling detail that anticipates her later style – seems already established. The subjects are also simple, graphic, often severe, and intensely poetic. But already one is sensing her emerging fascination and conversancy with an inner world and its store of traditional reference and meaning. Often one is quakingly aware that there are stories abroad, magic, spell-bound moments frozen from folk-tale with all their ambivalence of light and dark.

Not surprising then that later, perhaps triggered by commissions to illustrate, this familiarity with – and instinctive command of – folk and fairy tale became a dominant influence on much of her work. But even when this narrative sense informs her drawings, they are always more than illustrations. Often – even those which more recently might be thought to be glances back to her Catholic education – they achieve a feeling of captured momentary enchantment – quite disturbing, as if, true to the force of folk-tale, the survival of the world is in the balance. Her figures too, at first deceptive glance mannered, even a shade innocuous, are later discovered to be the closely observed, fully realised inhabitants of this ambiguous inner world, and so vehicles of taut, magical expression.

In her recent work she has increasingly been drawing with a brush. More colour, but still subdued as if to be true to the monochrome of some secret world of enchantment. The brush introduces a new freedom of line, and maybe achieves new dream-intensity for this real and imagined world.

Much is made of a woman's capacity for "multi-tasking". But with Truda Lane there is a singleness that unifies the vocations of housewife and artist that are usually assumed to be at odds. A discipline, economy, almost an austerity, that finds meaning through unremitting, unquestioned practice. A constancy that extends to her enduring, and surely symbiotic relationship with Resurgence Magazine. These are qualities that one might expect to show in an unyielding, hard-edged style. One is quite taken aback to find the contrary – a line so intensely felt it appears natural, in fact something of nature, and alive with an untoiled sense of devotion.

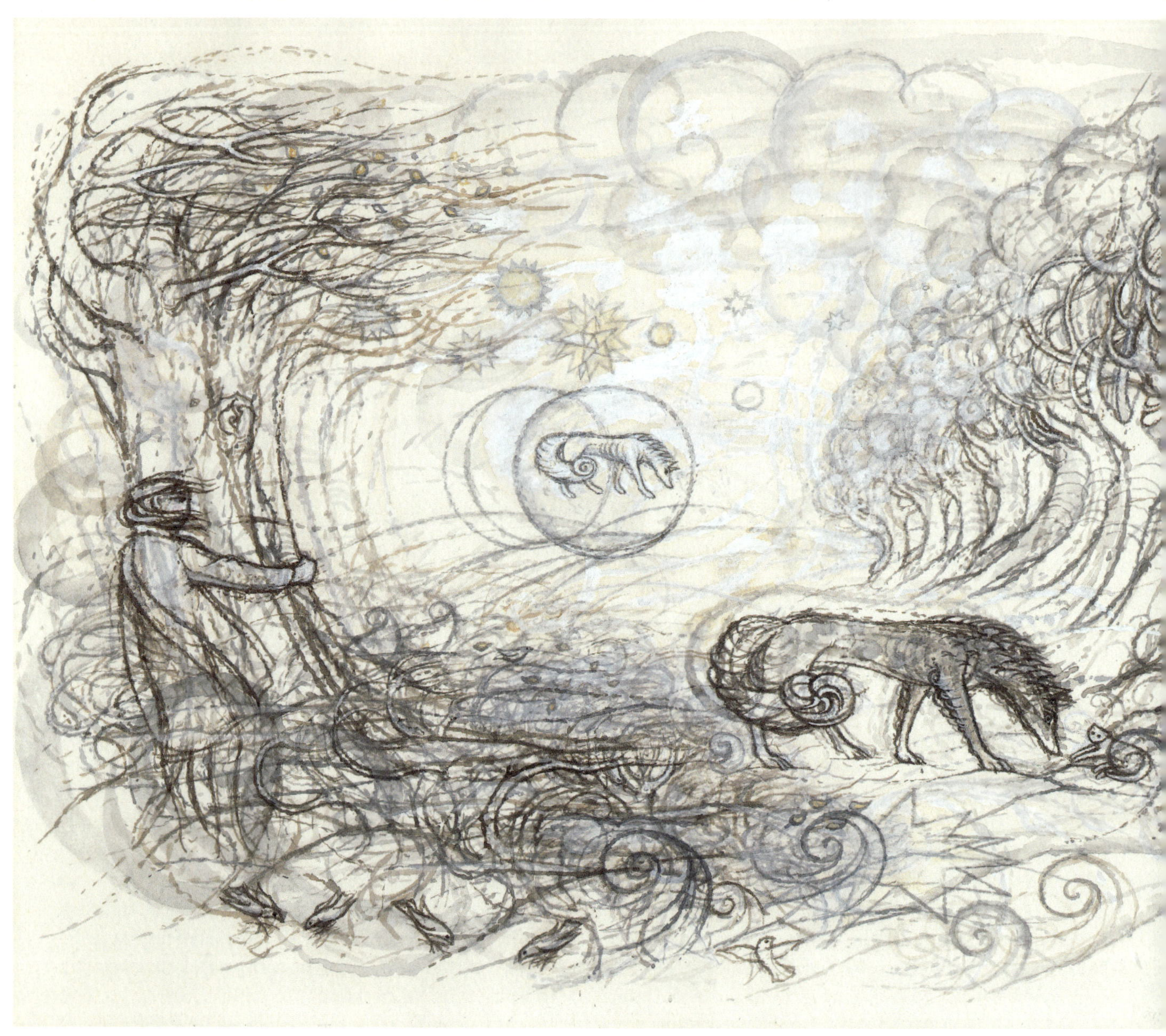

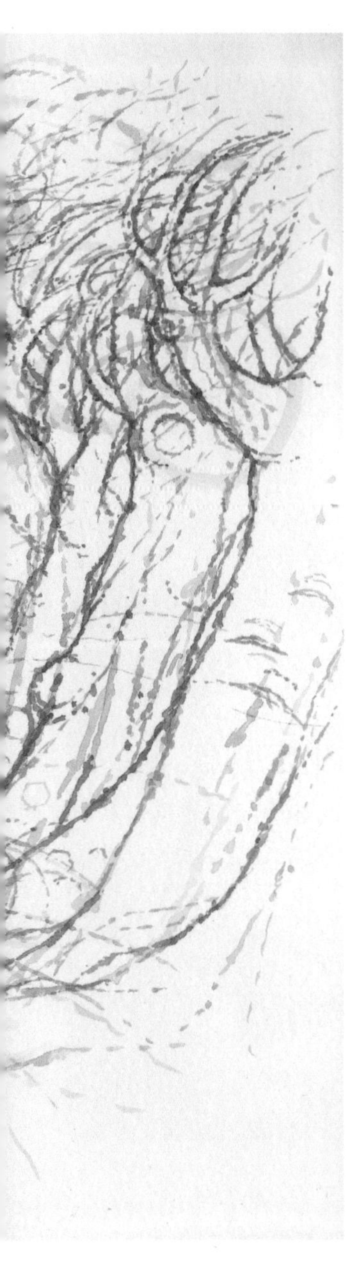

# CONTENTS

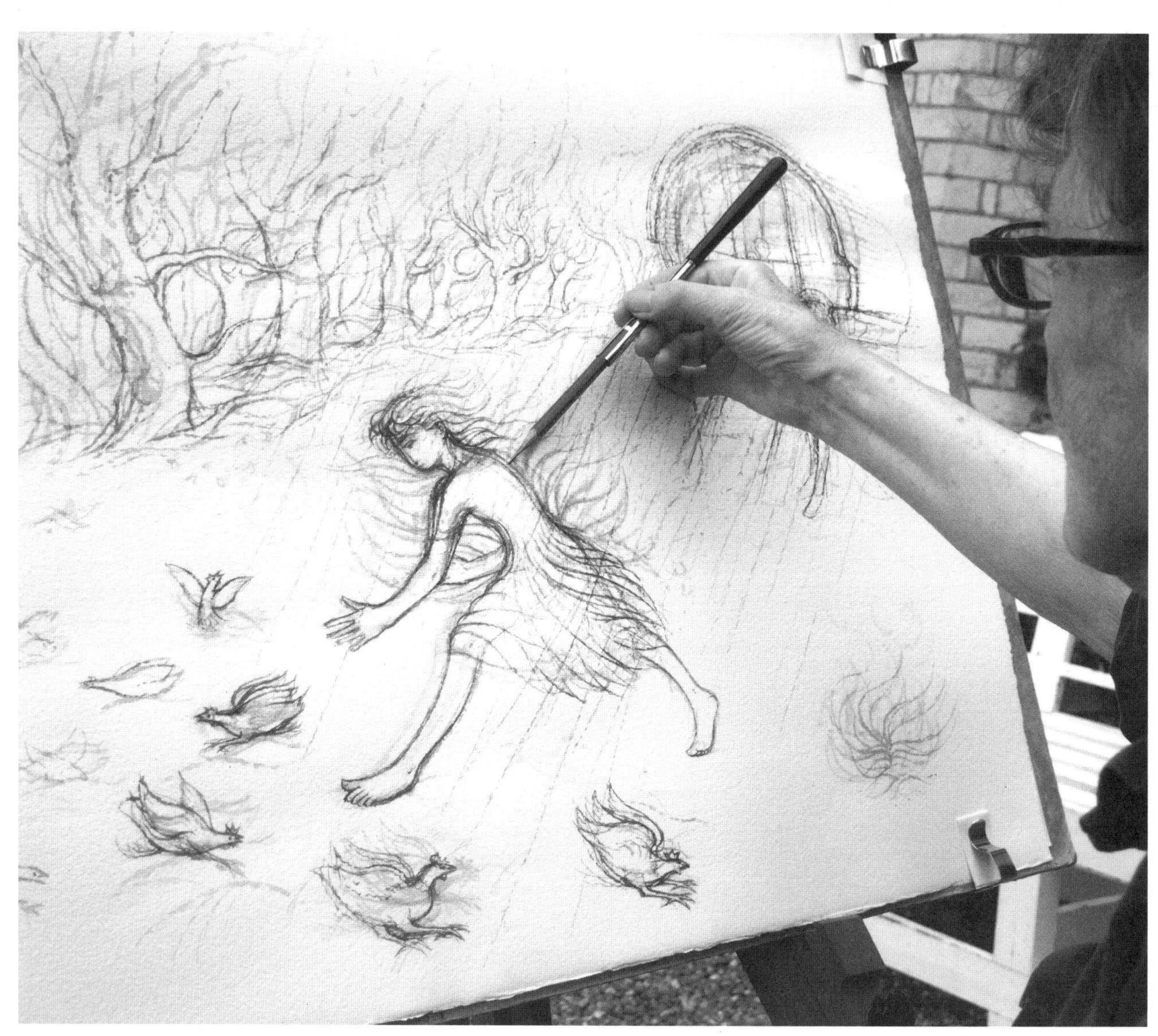

Truda Lane drawing 2010, photographed by Nat Lane.

# INTRODUCTION
## by Truda Lane

If asked, "How would you define a good drawing?", I would say, "One that you can set bones from", i.e. broken bones.

Structure is endlessly and eternally fascinating: here lies the source of life, dynamic energy and movement.

Most of my imaginative works are inspired by something seen or experienced; sometimes stored in the mind for a number of years.

I have been inspired by mythology, poetry, folk and fairytale, but in representing these things I never lose sight of the objective study of natural forms – trees, people, animals, birds, plant forms etc. One is always looking, searching and discovering, and without objective study the imaginative work will founder.

It has been quite rightly observed that as much imagination is needed to draw something one can see, as to make something up.

John Ruskin wrote about drawing: "The greatest thing a human soul ever does in this world is to see something and to tell what it saw in a plain way … to see clearly is poetry, prophecy and religion all in one."

I cannot write anything better than this. What Ruskin calls "a plain way" of seeing and drawing I see as economy, clarity and a penetrating observation of all wild and natural things: these are my inspiration, and without them I can do nothing.

# MYTHOLOGY

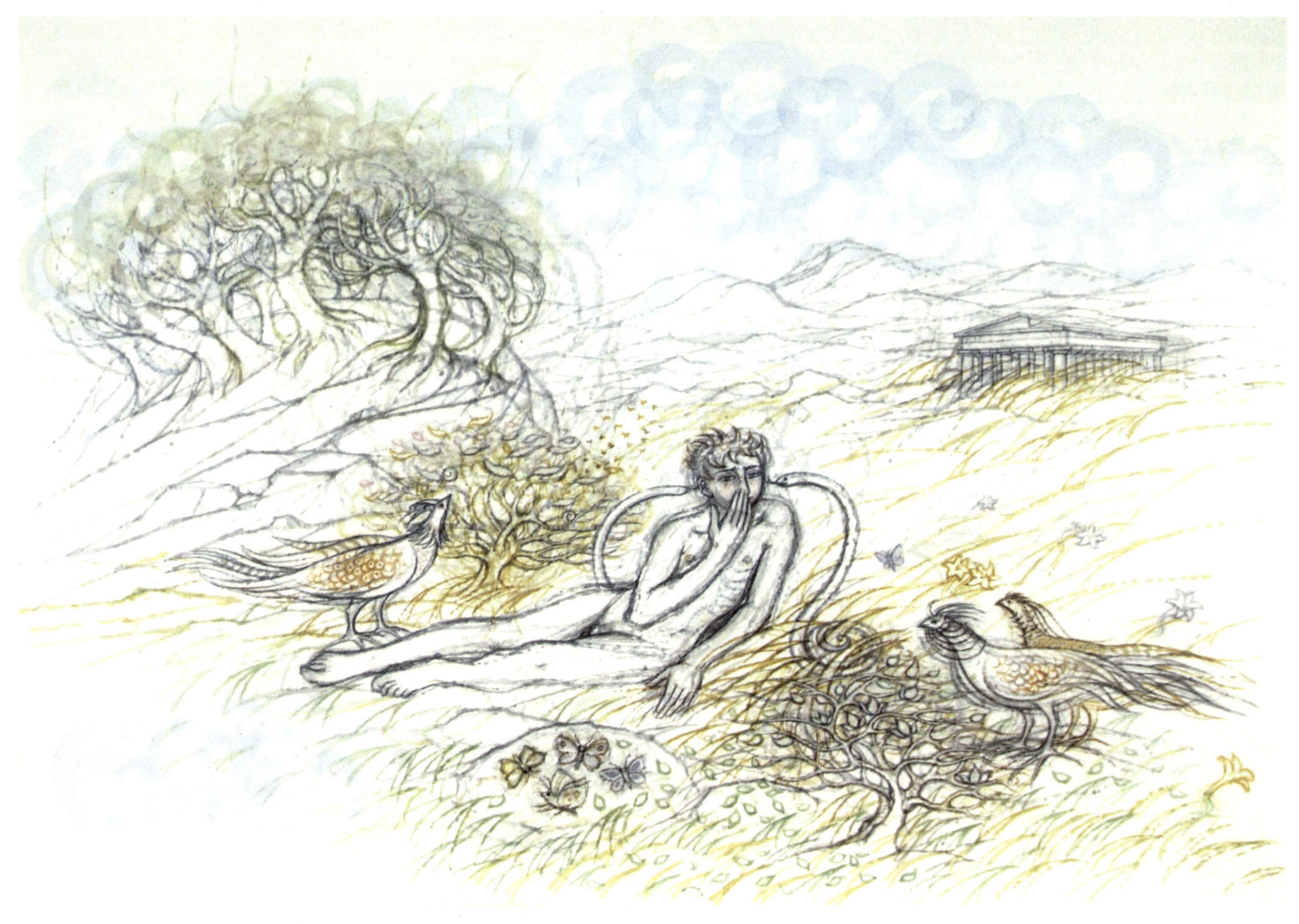

In the archaic Greek story "Melampus", a young boy buries a dead serpent; her children, by licking his ears reward him with the gift of knowing all animal speech, including that of insects and of birds.

**Melampus**
brush/watercolour
55 x 77 cm

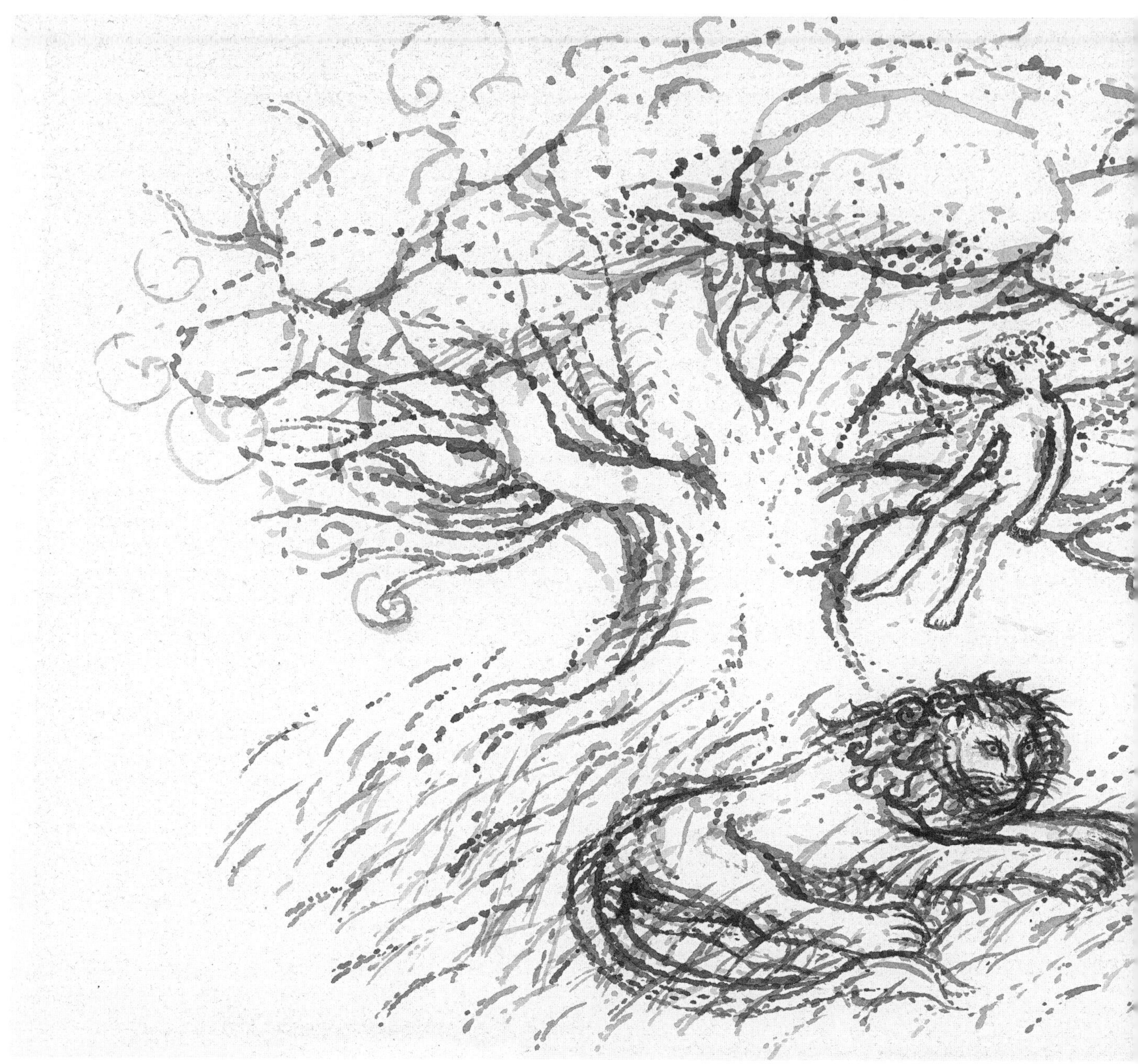

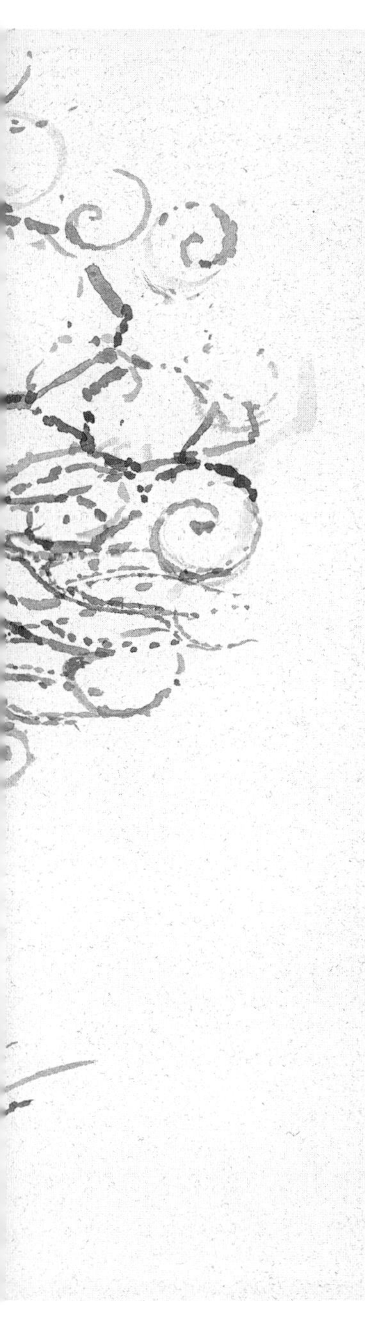

The old lion longs to grasp the young creature, but it is out of reach.

**Youth and Age:** an allegory
brush/watercolour
24 x 35 cm

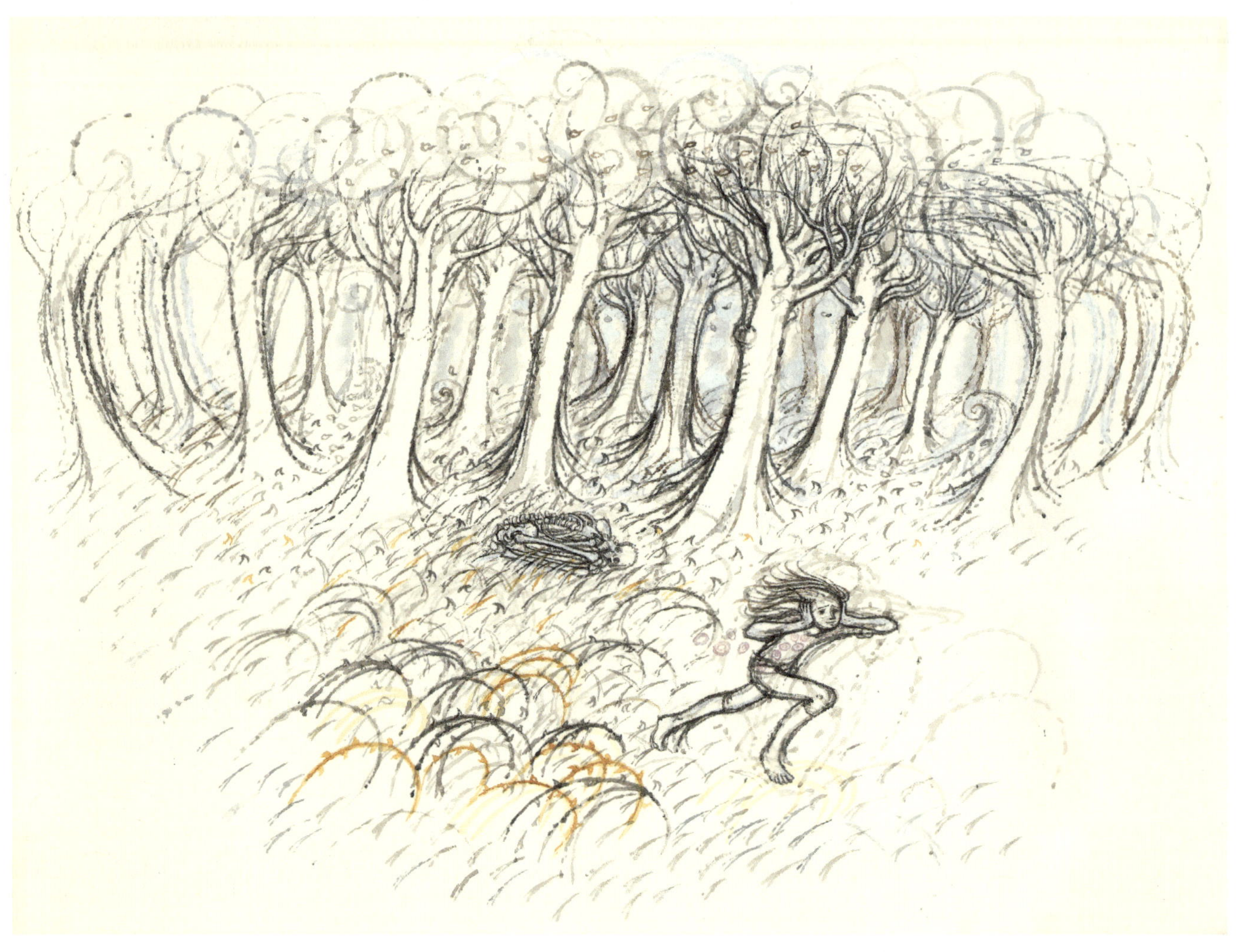

**The Dark Wood**

brush/watercolour

43 x 57 cm

The dark wood as a symbol of the wide world.

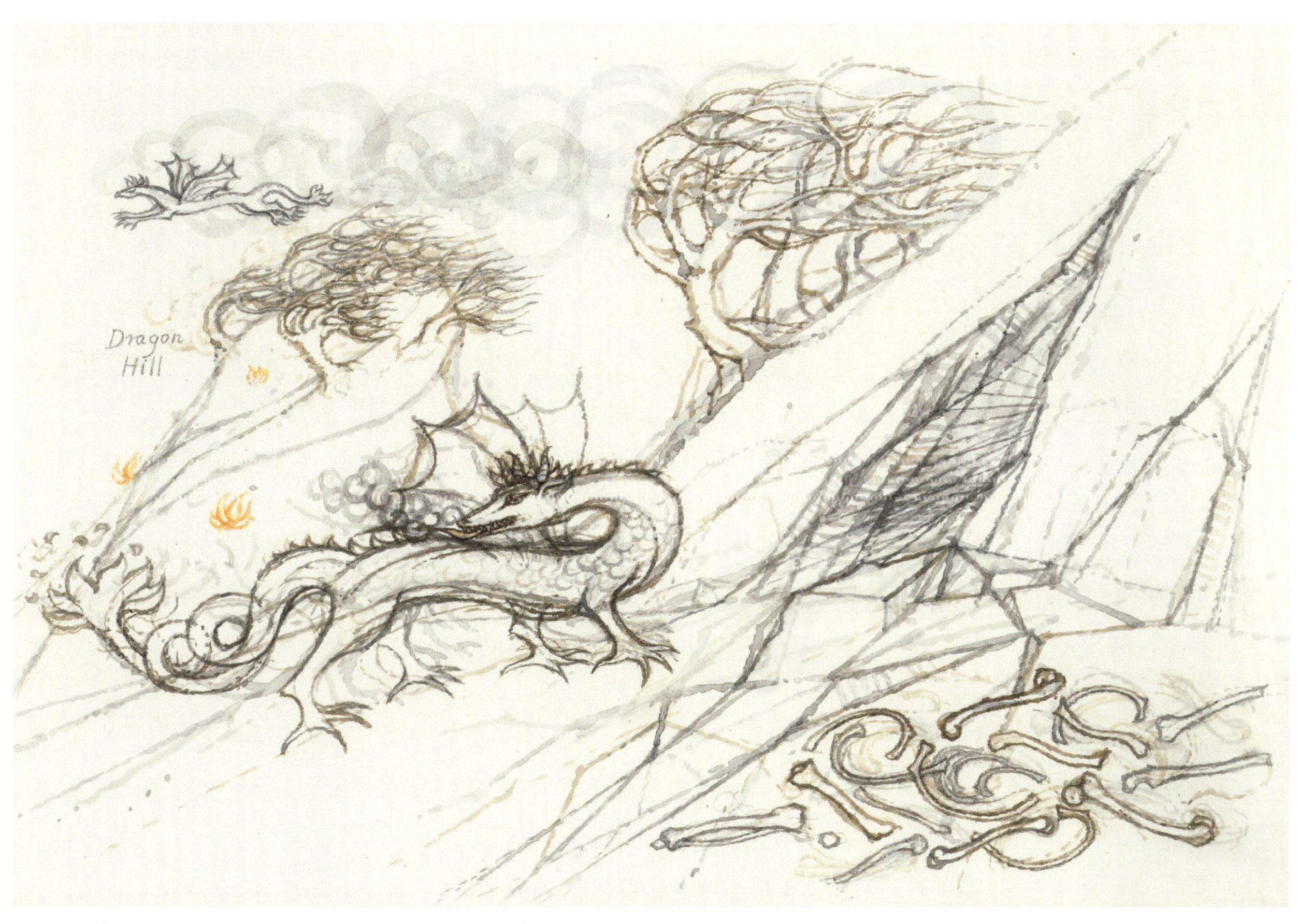


**Dragon preening itself**

watercolour

37.5 x 55 cm

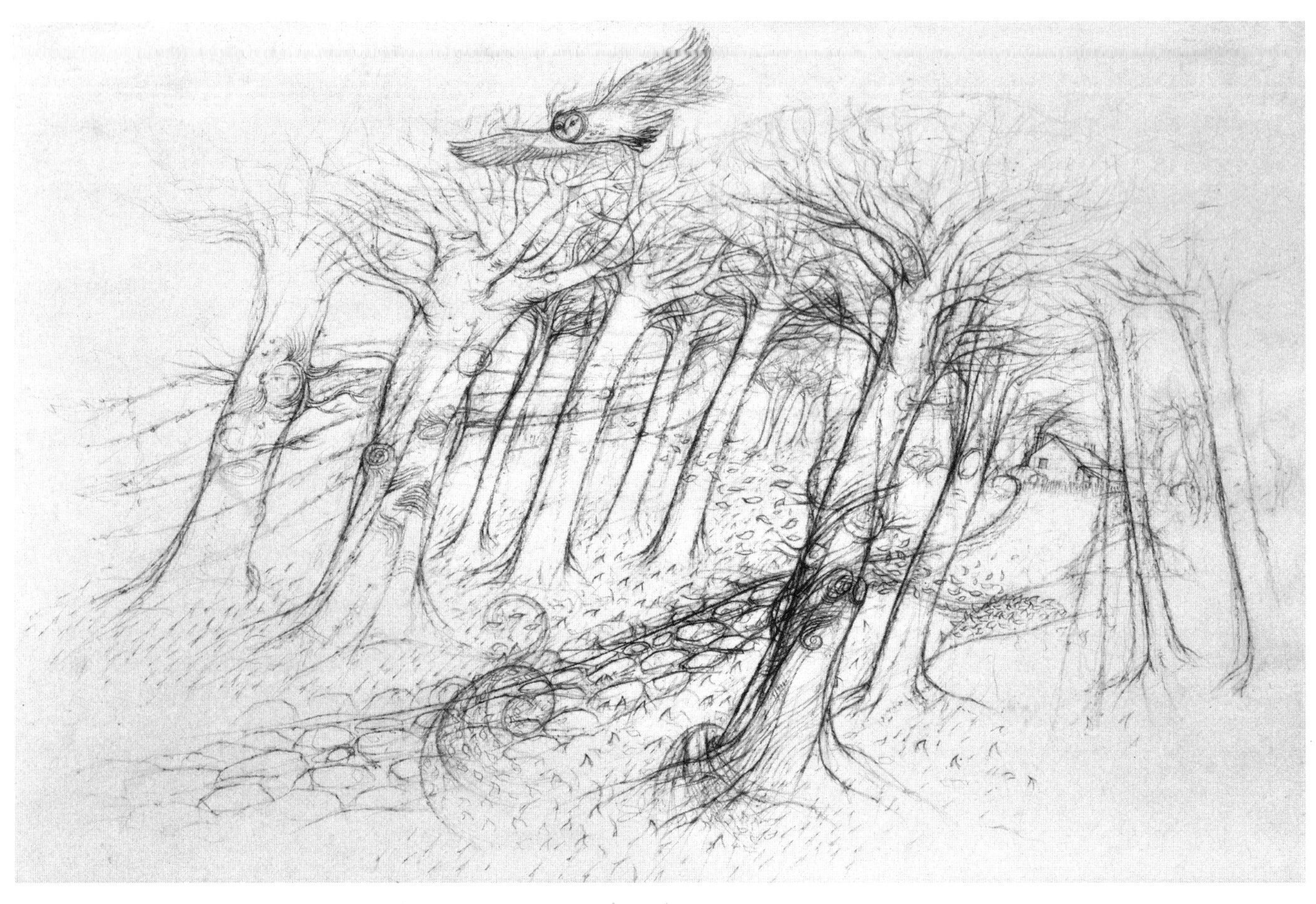

**The Road**
pencil
55 x 76 cm

Inspired by Walter de la Mare's poem "The Owl".
Collection of poems "The Burning - Glass".

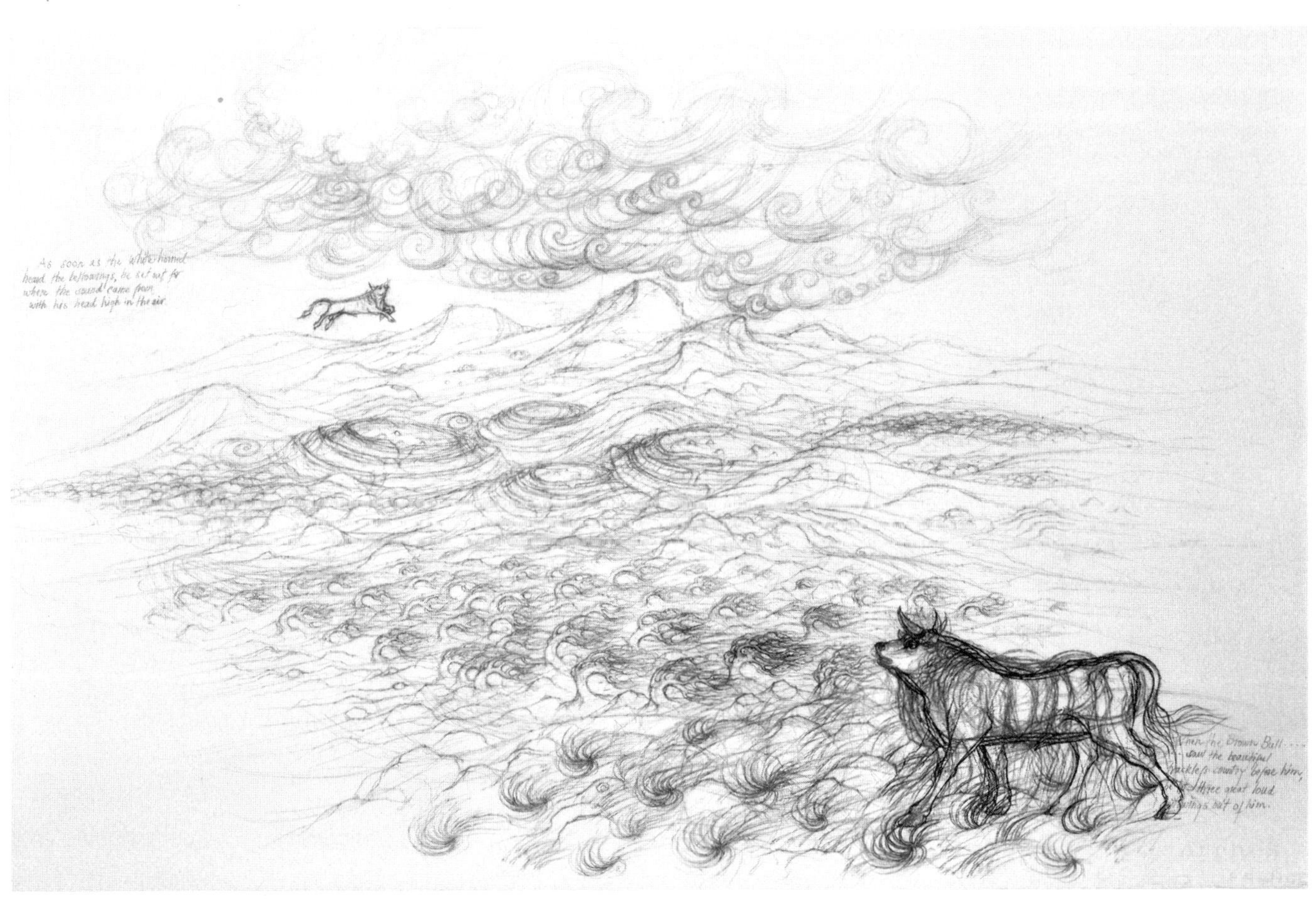


Inspired by the Irish epic "Táin Bó Cuailnge", translated by Thomas Kinsella.

**The Brown Bull of Ulster and the White Bull of Connaught**

pencil and indian ink

48 x 71 cm

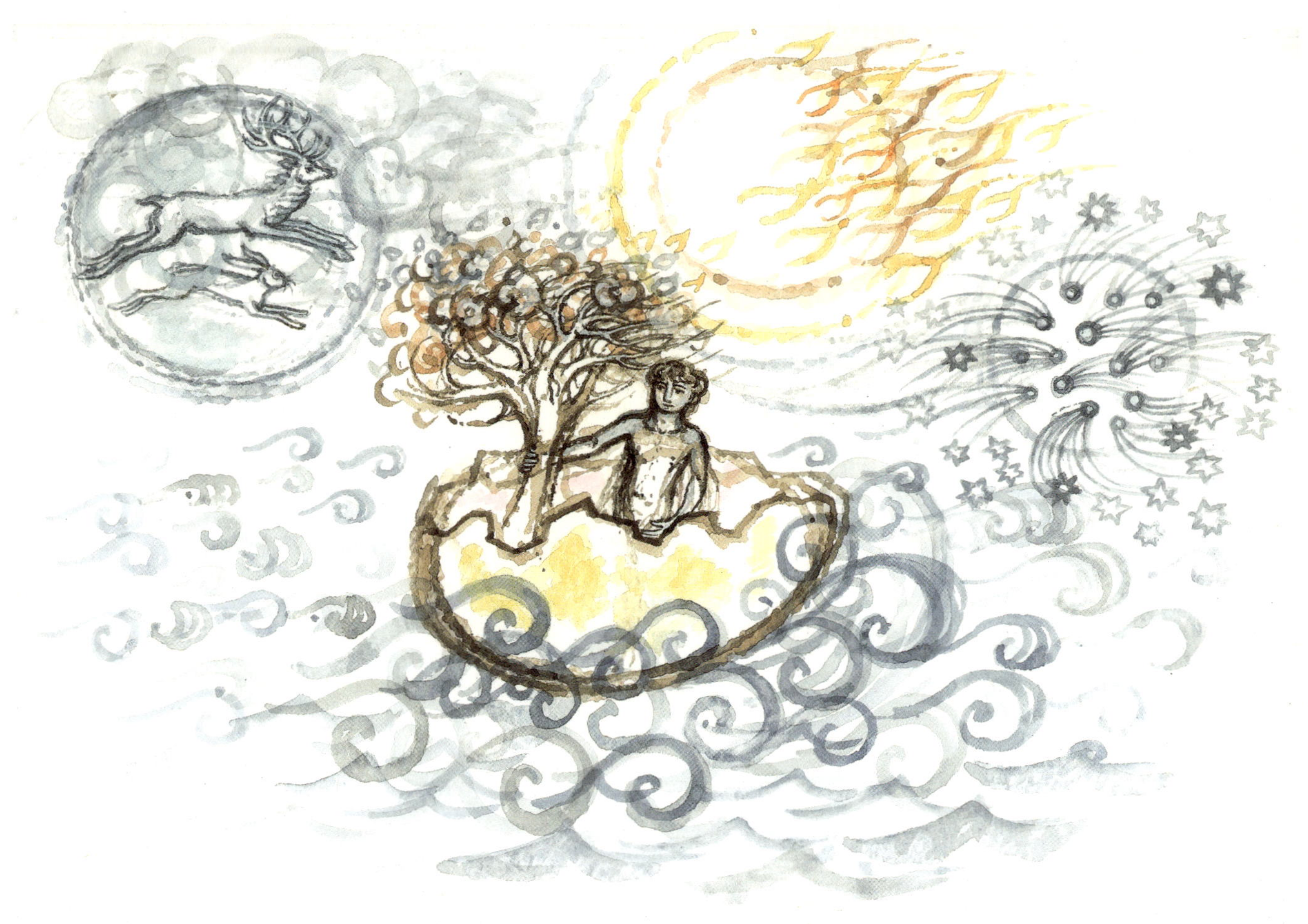

**Creation Myth**
(Resurgence)
watercolour
25 x 35 cm

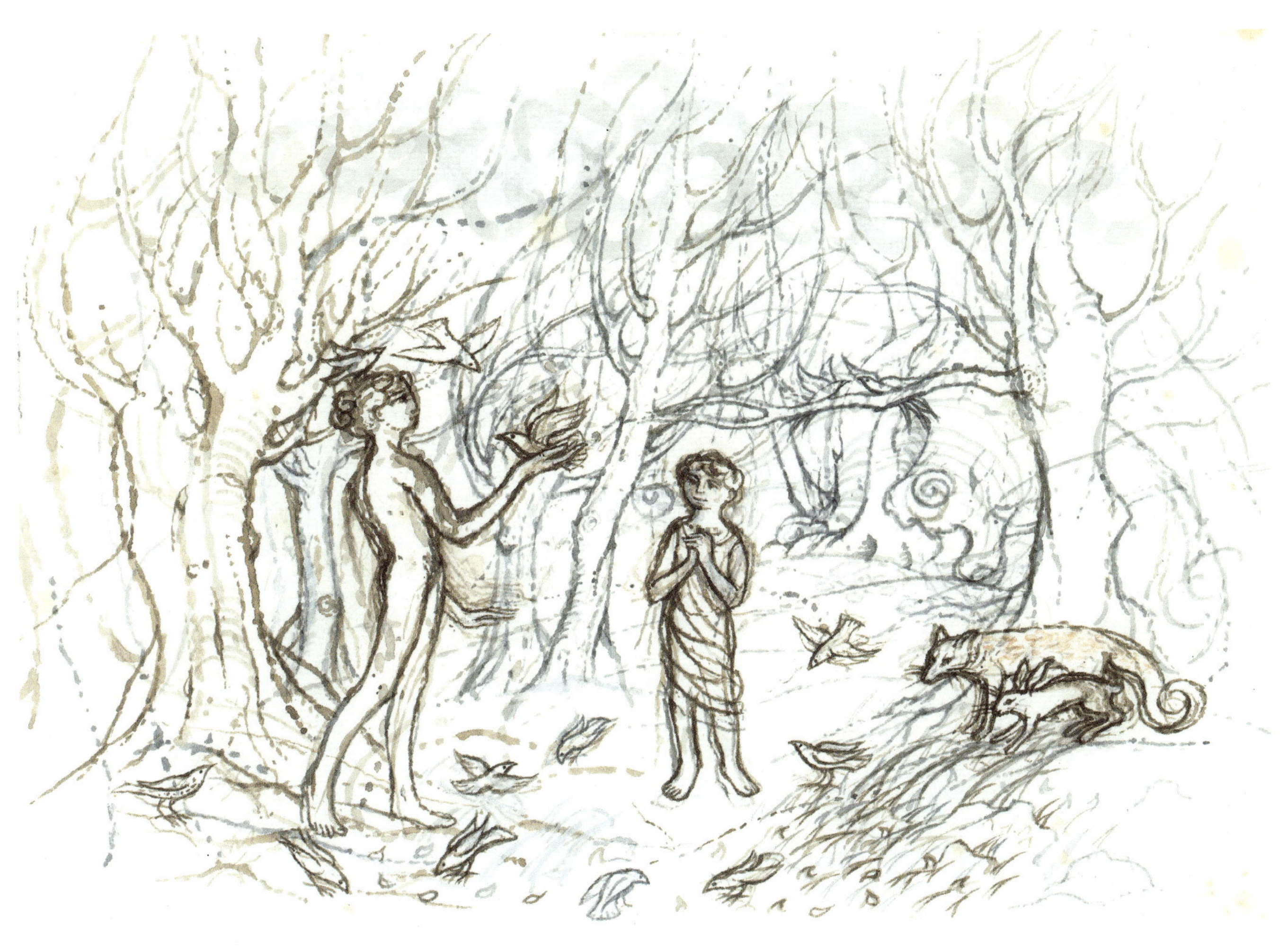

**The Bird Goddess:**
the peacable kingdom
watercolour
25 x 33 cm

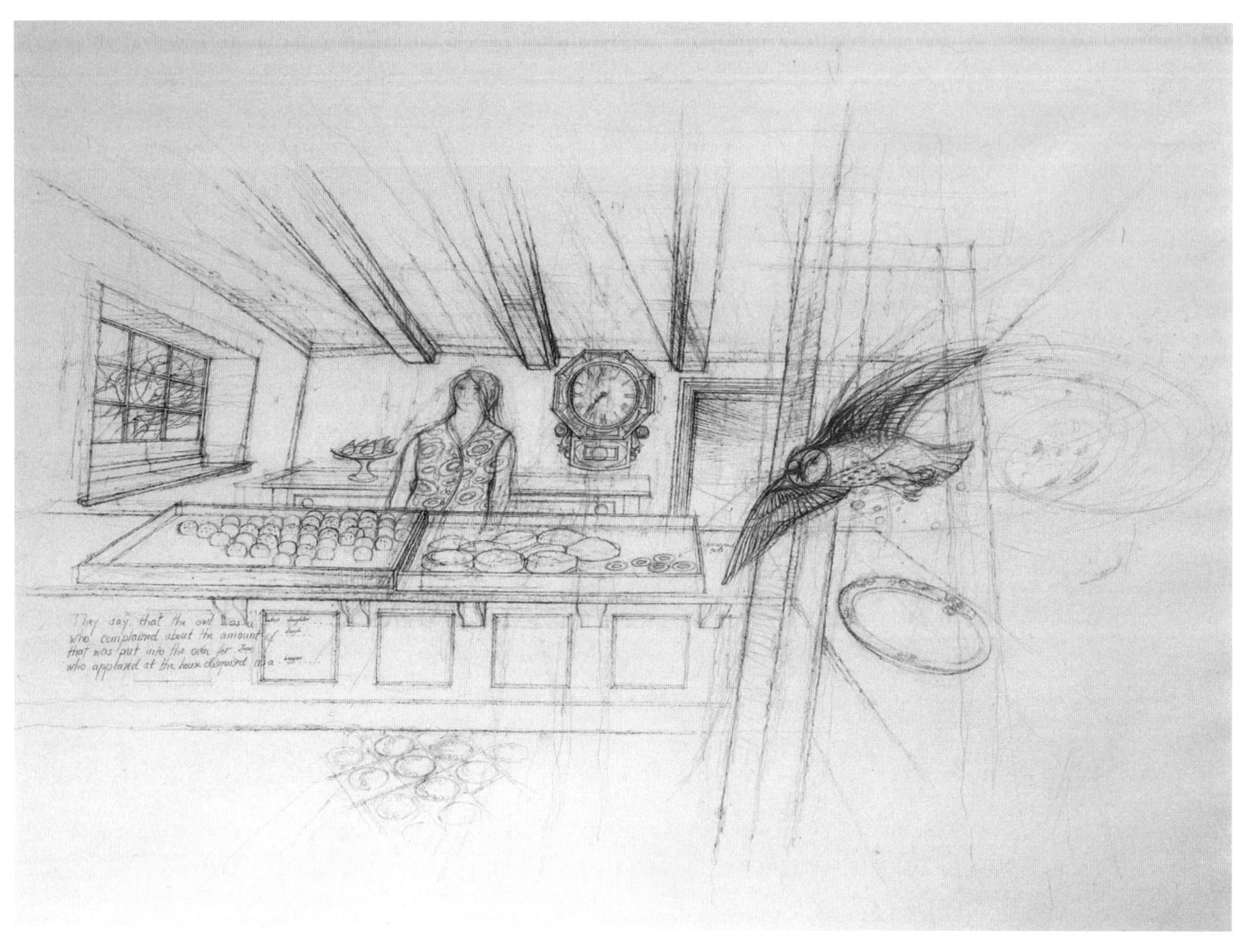


**They say the owl was a baker's daughter ...**

pencil

54 x 70 cm

The baker's daughter objected to the size of the dough put into the oven for Christ when he appeared at the house as a beggar, referred to by Shakespeare in "Hamlet". For full story see "Come Hither" by Walter de le Mare.

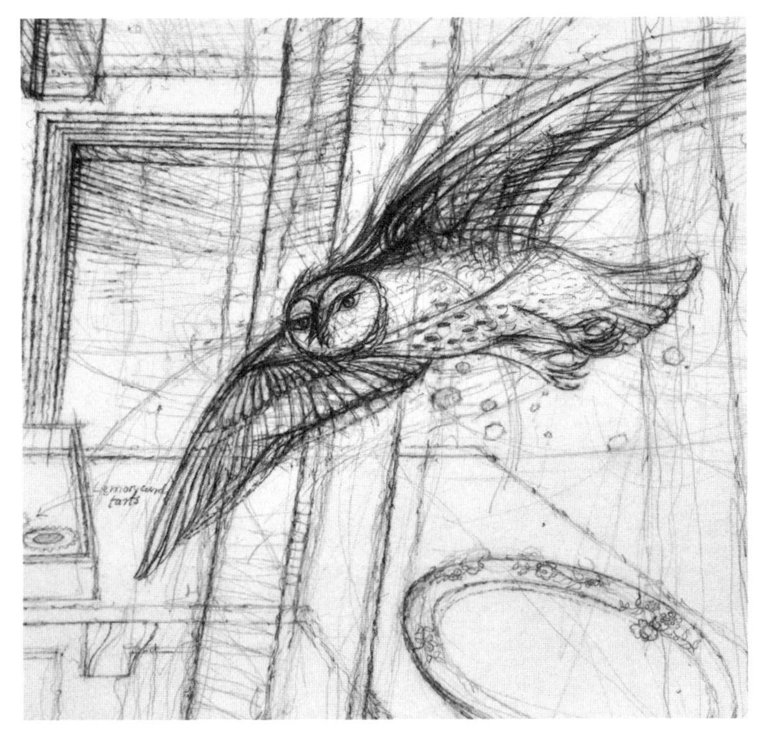


**They say the owl was a baker's daughter …**
(detail)

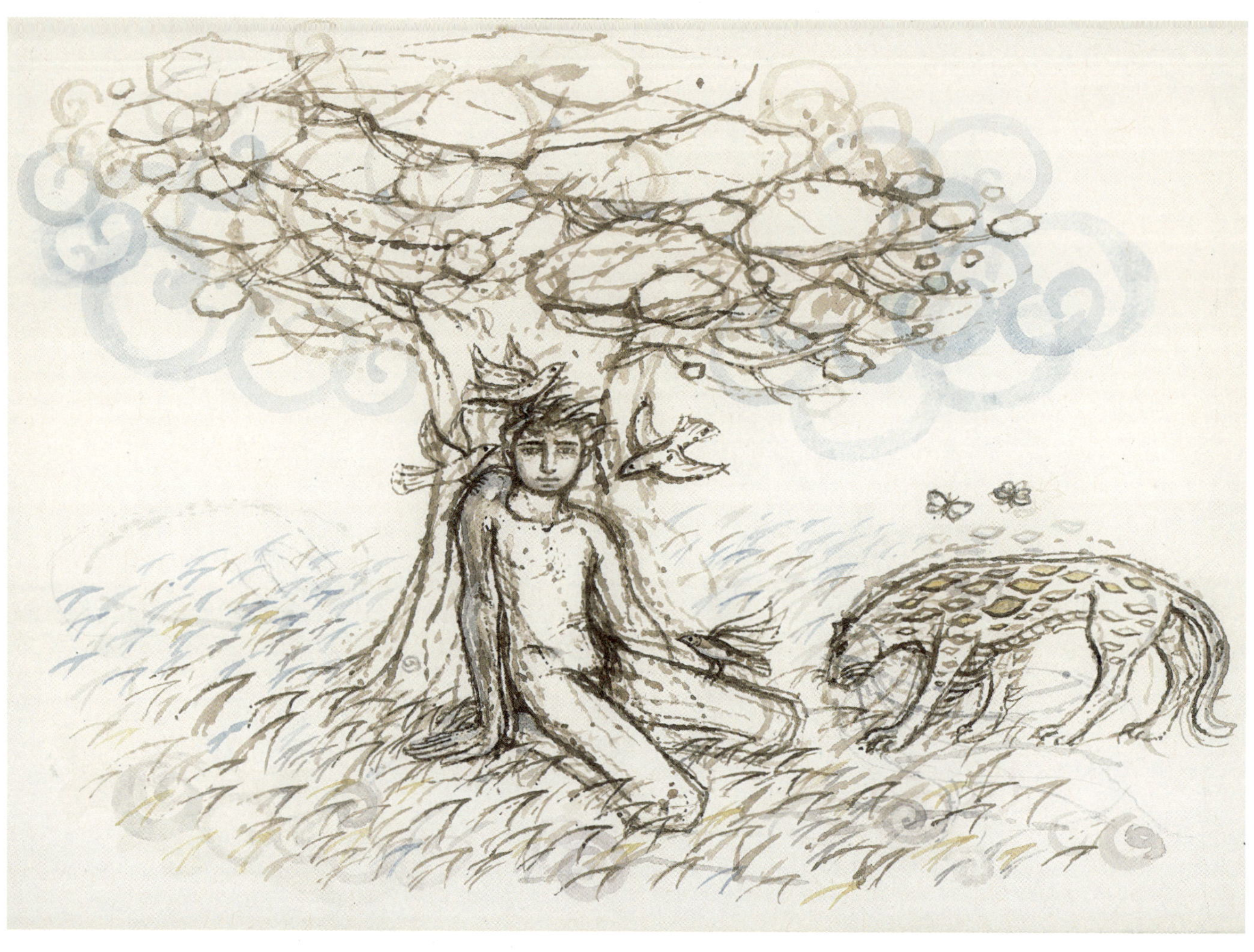

**Aengus**
(Resurgence)
watercolour
27 x 38 cm

The young man is Aengus, the Celtic god of youth. He was always accompanied by four birds.

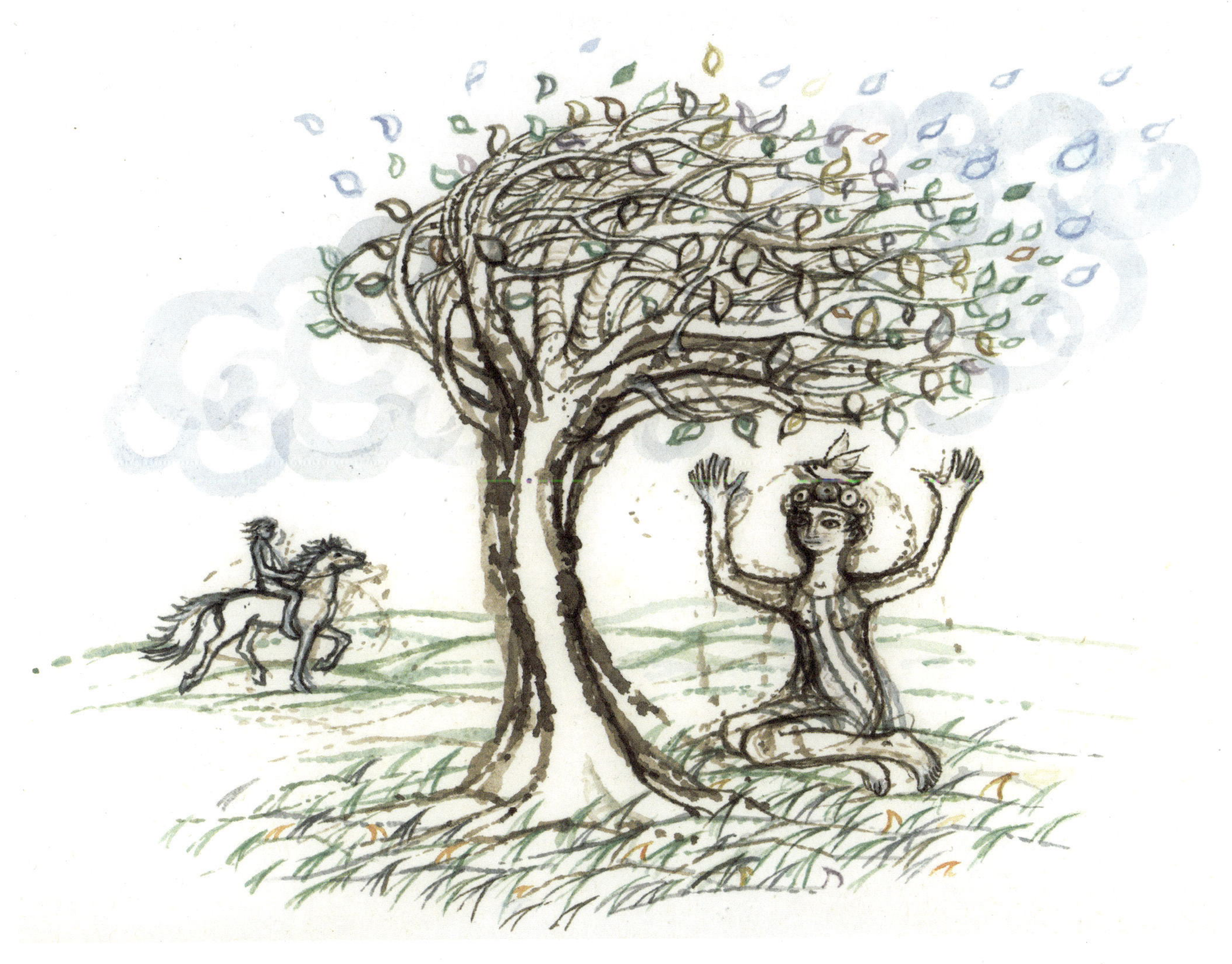

**The Singing Ringing Tree**
watercolour
29.5 x 39 cm

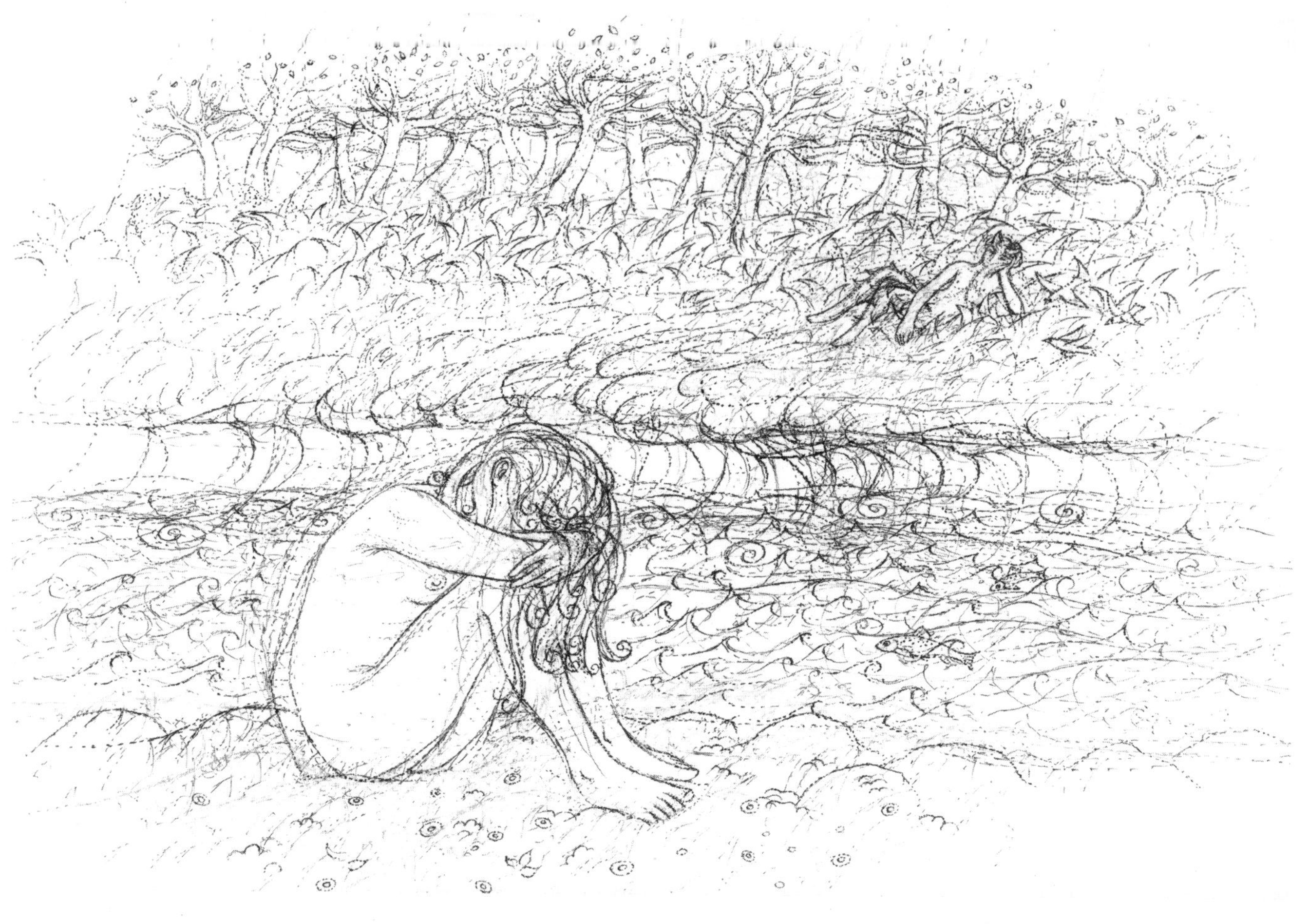

**Smoke:**
for a story by John Moat
indian ink
32 x 45.5 cm

A shy nymph awaits her equally shy beloved.

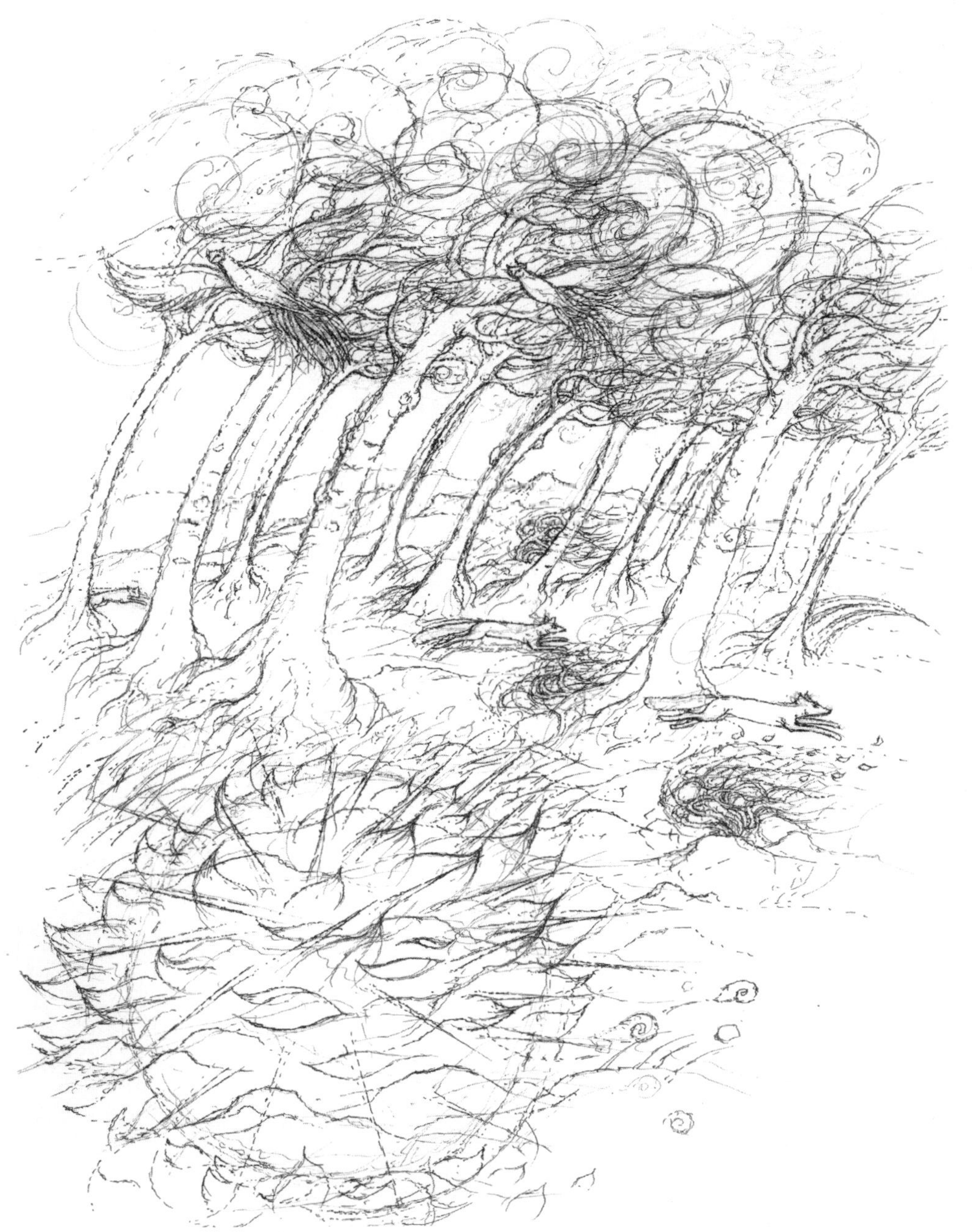

The Winter sun buried in the earth. North American Indian tradition.

**Winter Solstice**
(Resurgence)
indian ink
39 x 29 cm

# GARDENS

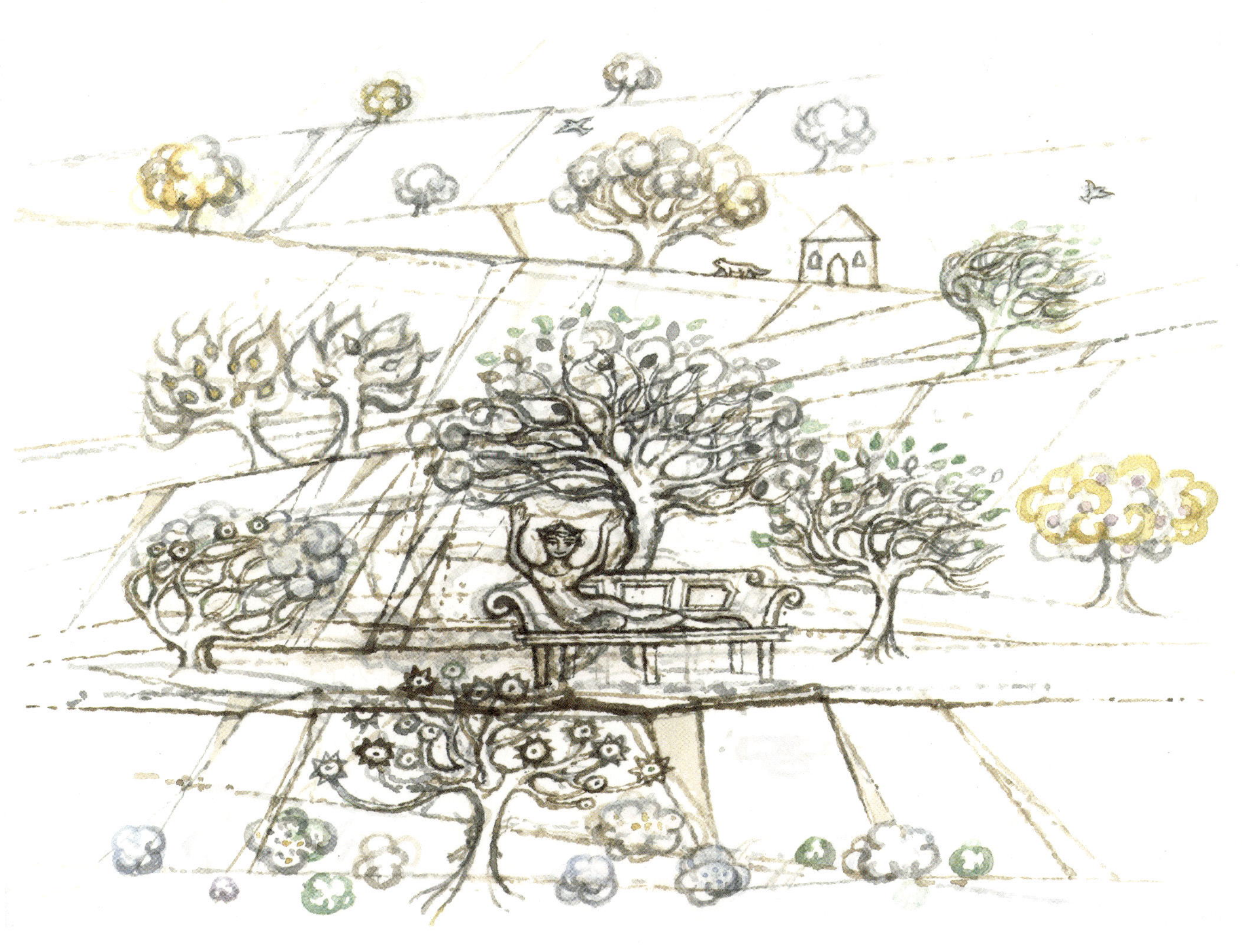

**Hanging Gardens of Babylon**

watercolour

23 x 30.5 cm

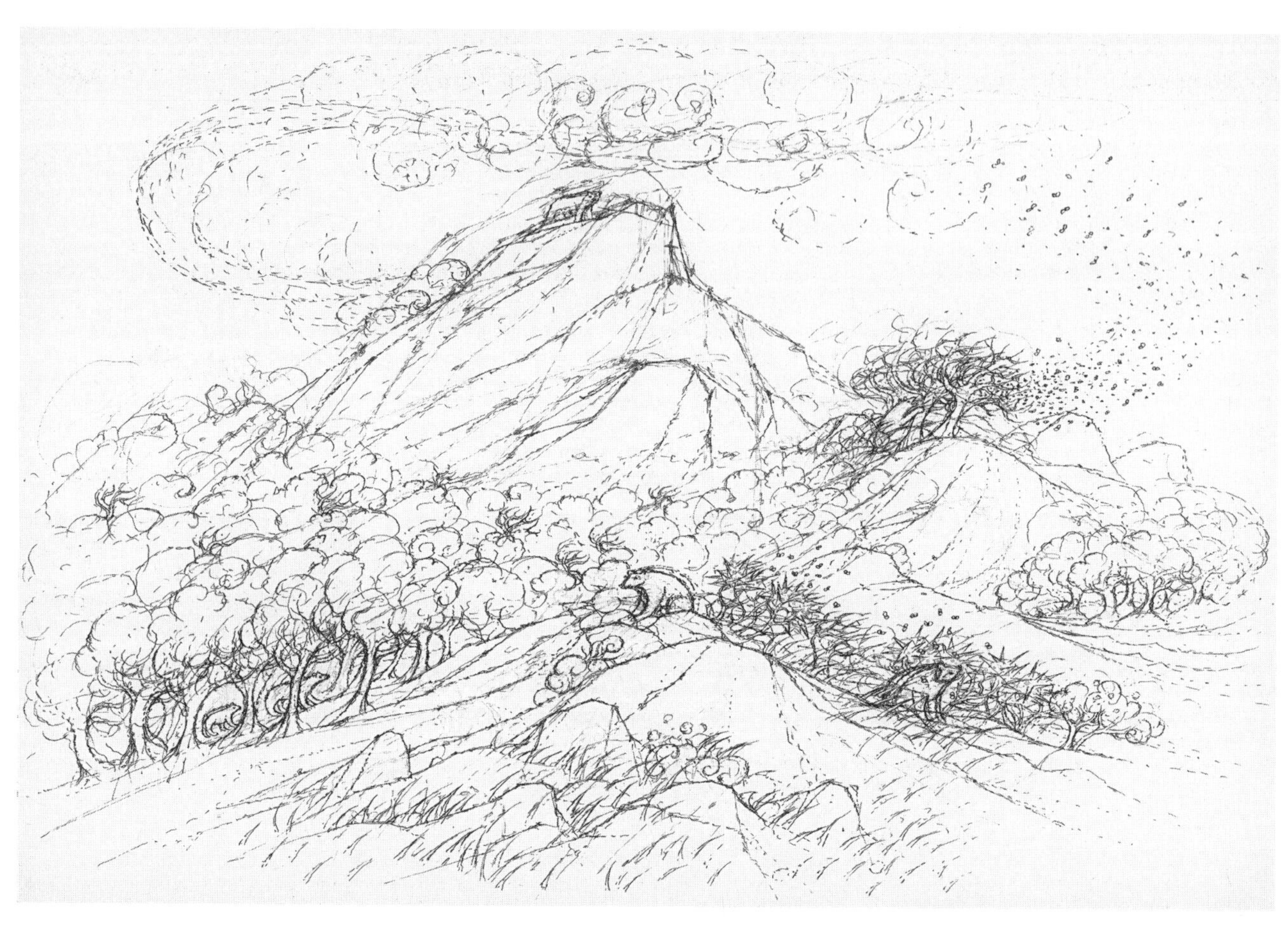

**A Bear Garden**

indian ink

22 x 32 cm

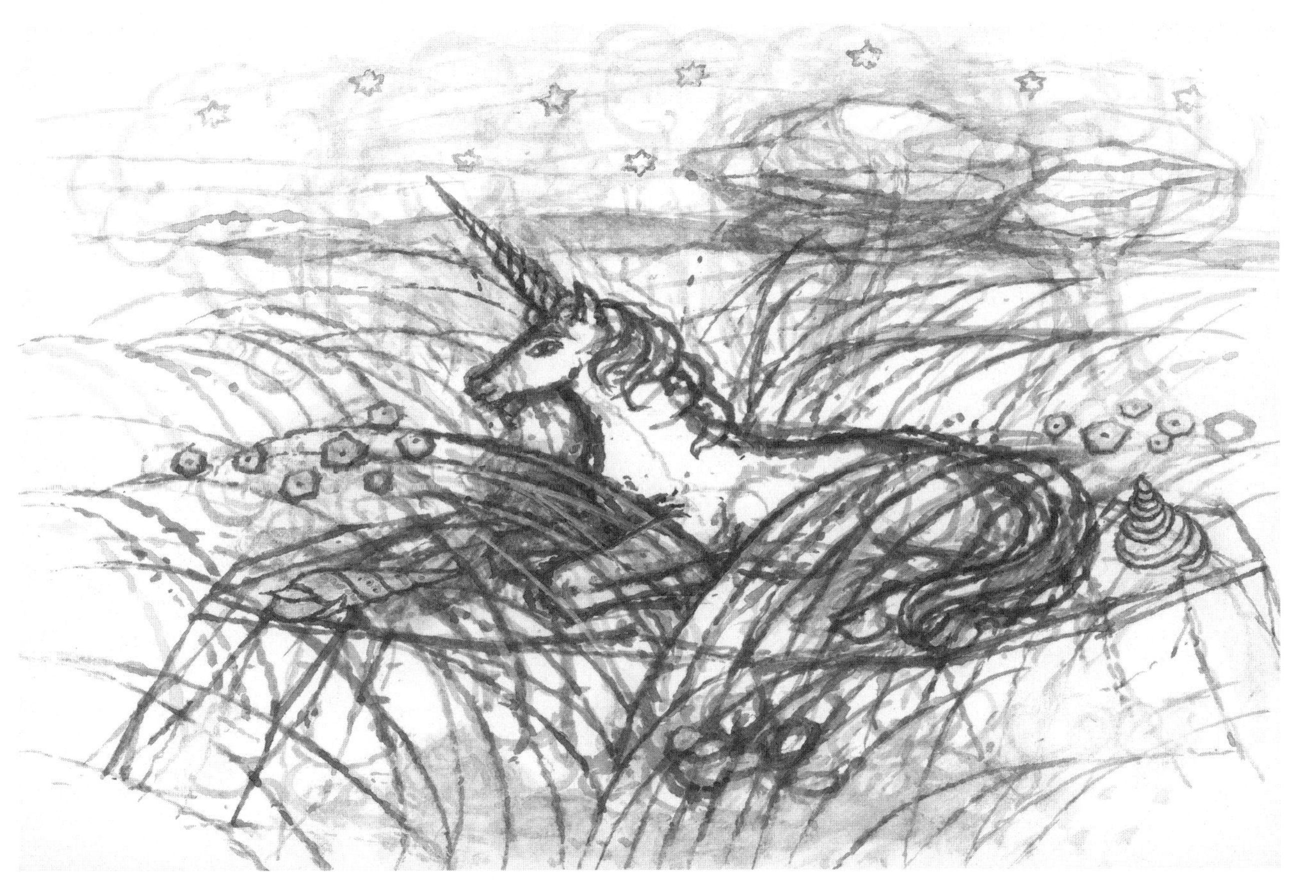

Inspired by a carved stone unicorn reclining on a plinth in the garden of Cothay Manor, Somerset.

**The Unicorn**
watercolour
14.5 x 21.5 cm

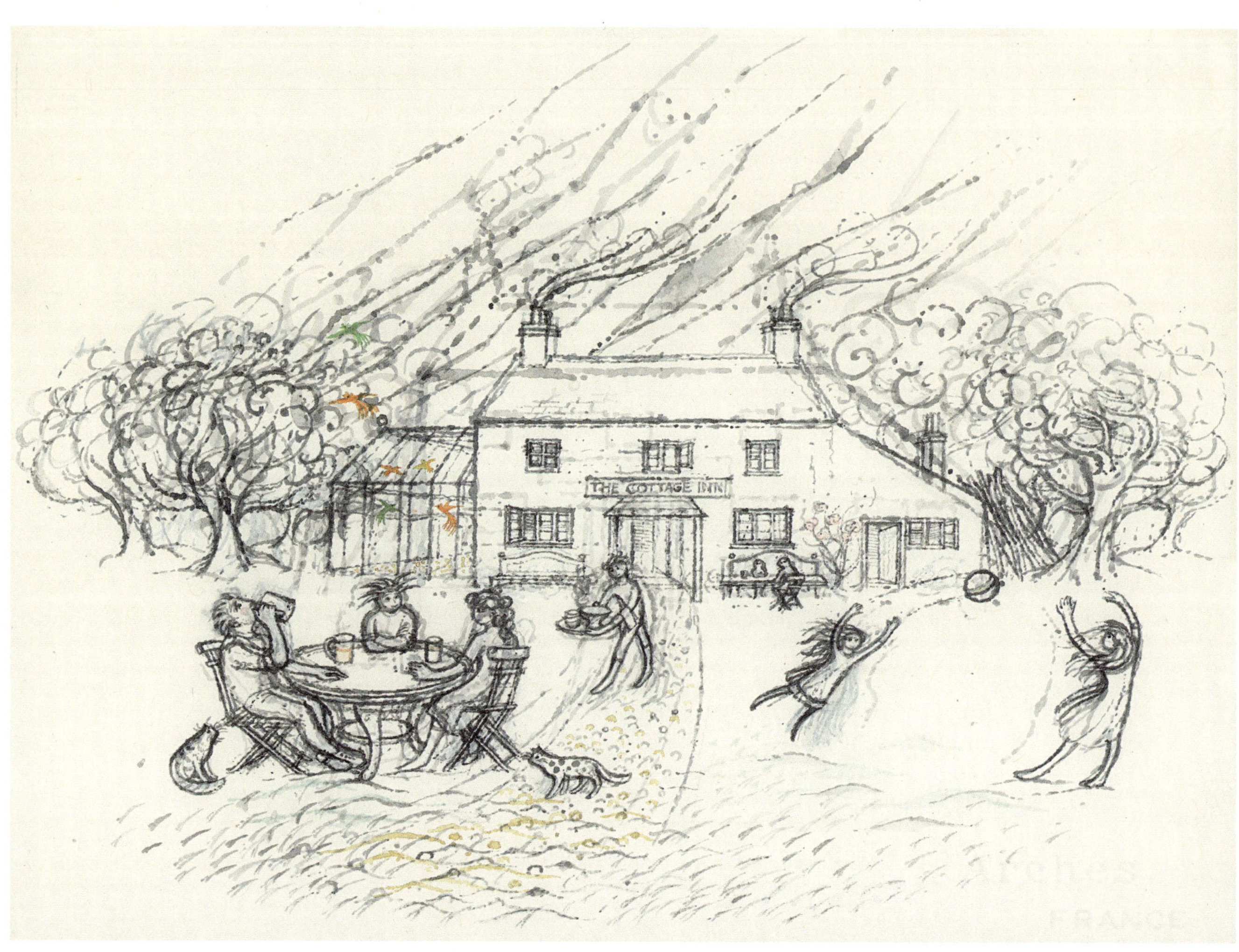


**Beer Garden:**

The Cottage Inn

watercolour

30 x 38 cm

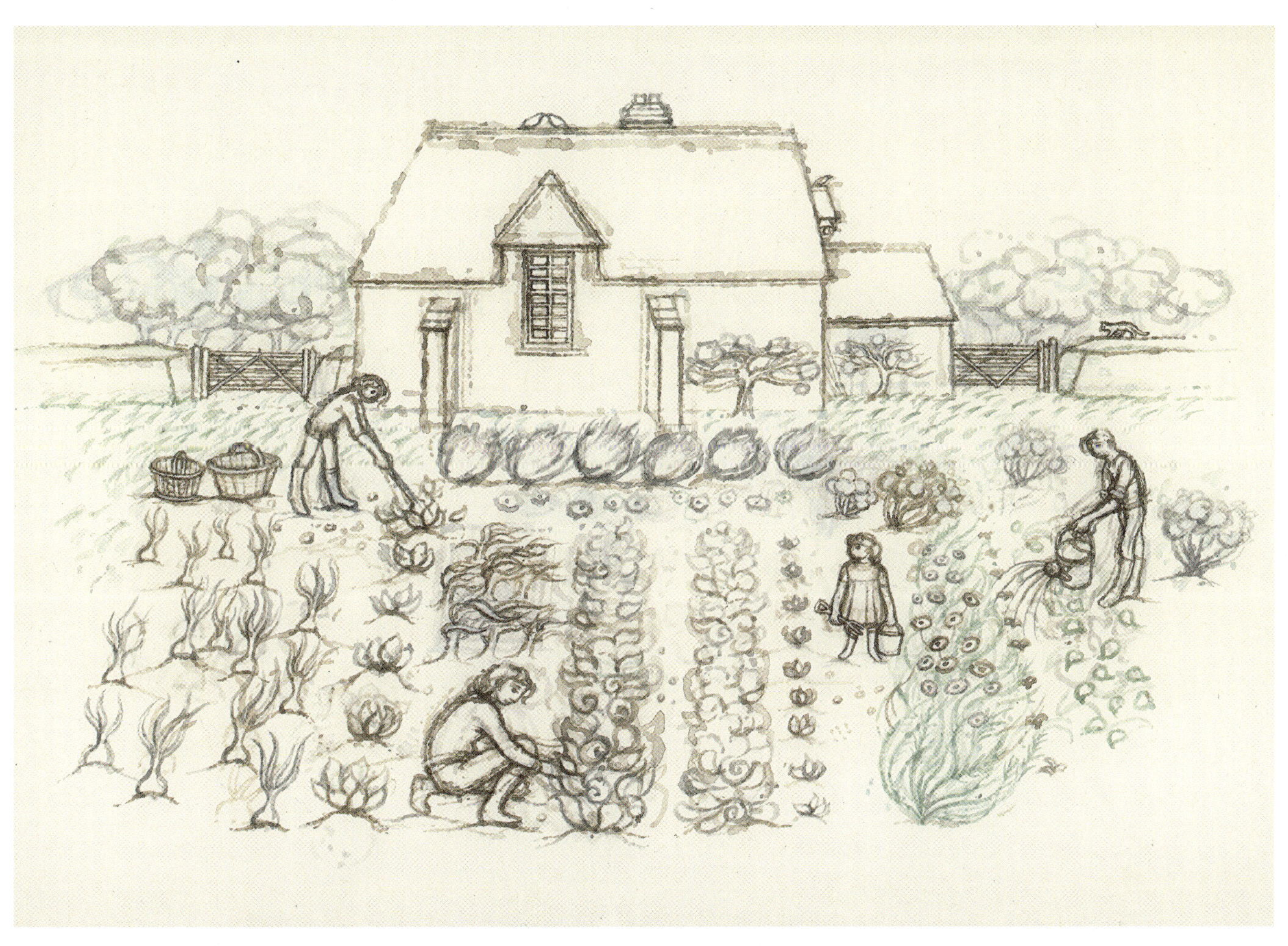

**Small School Garden**
(Resurgence)
watercolour
24 x 34 cm

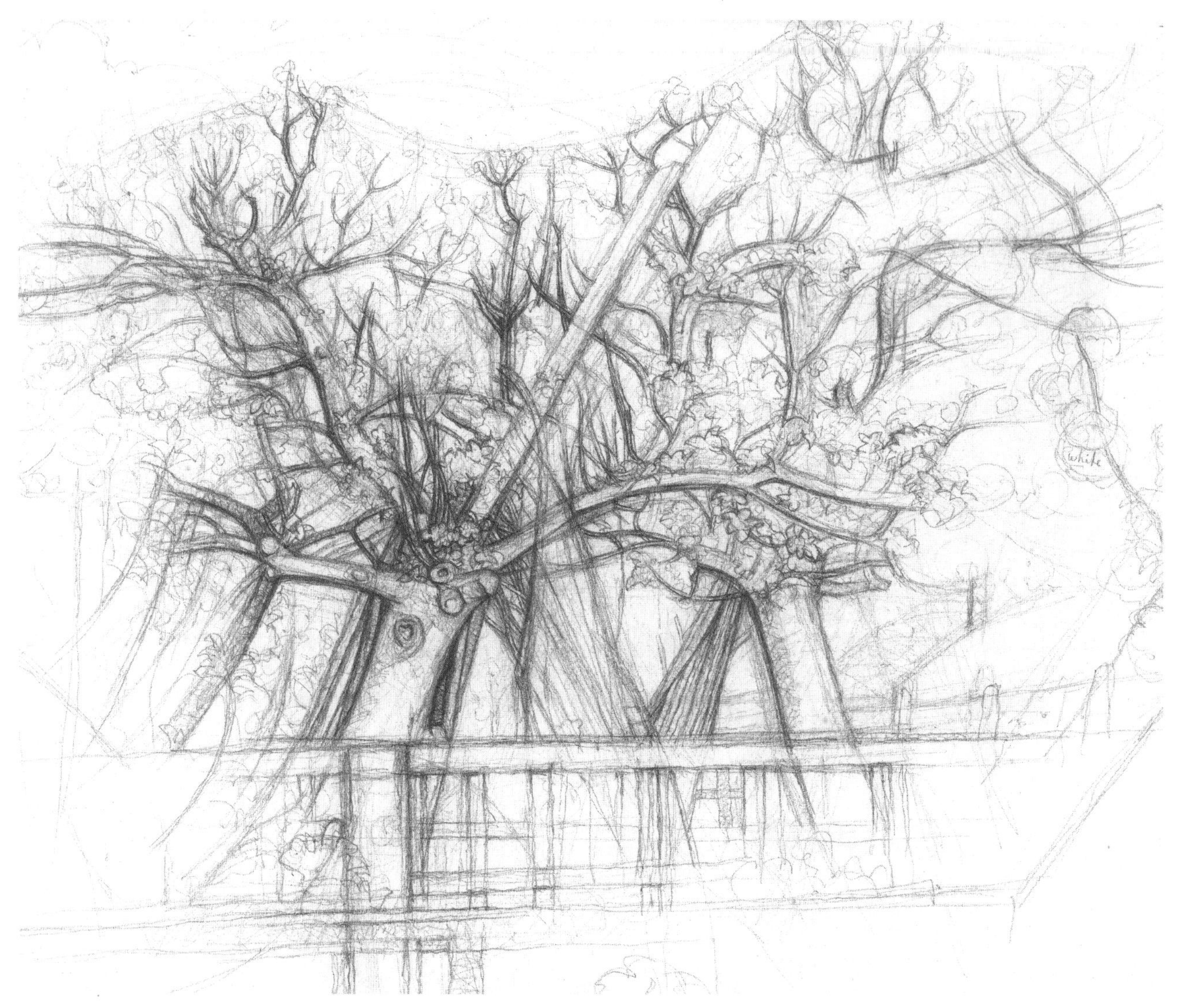


**Fruit trees in a back garden**
Early drawing
pencil
29 x 33 cm

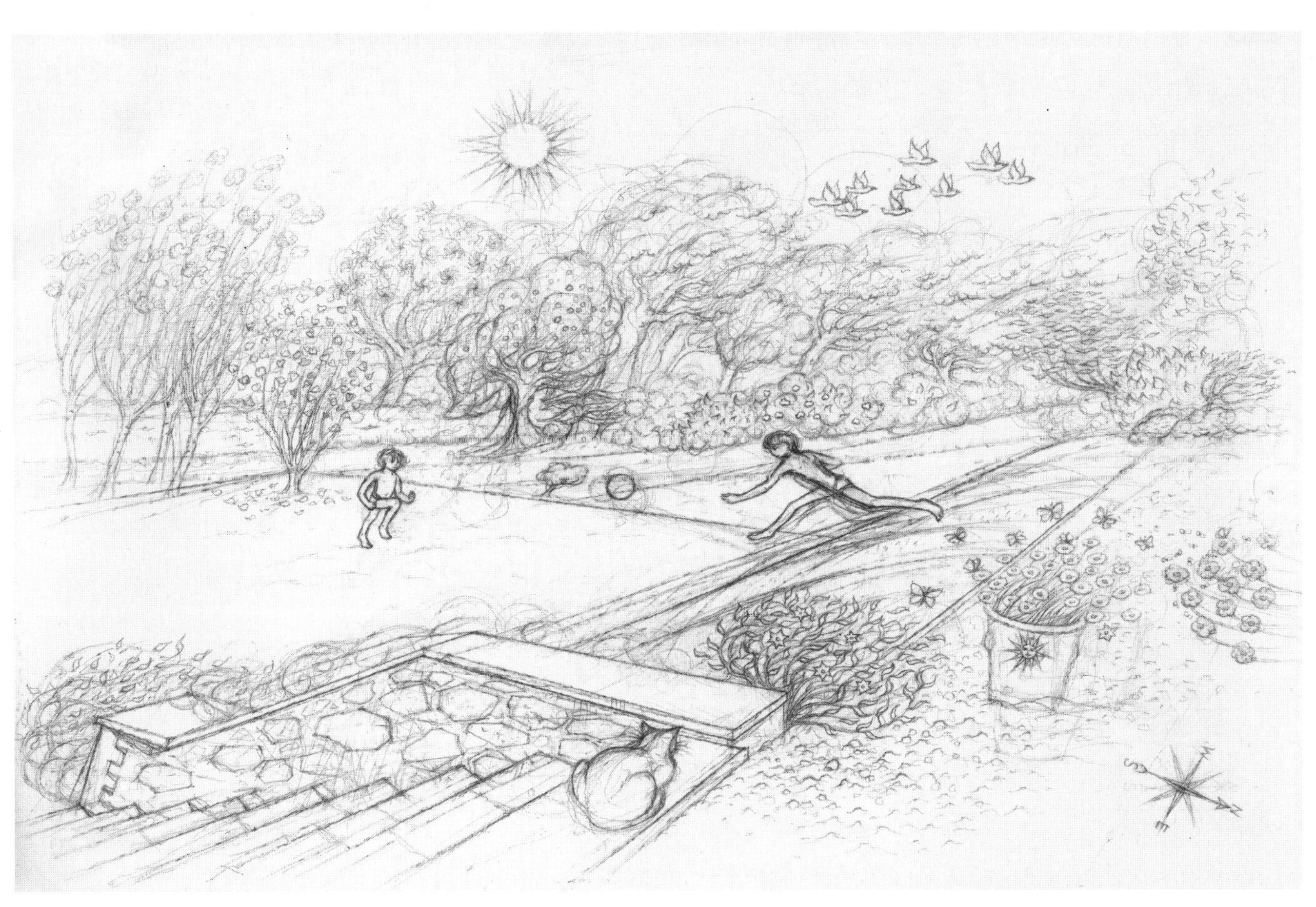

**Children's garden:**
Toby and Oliver
pencil
38 x 57 cm

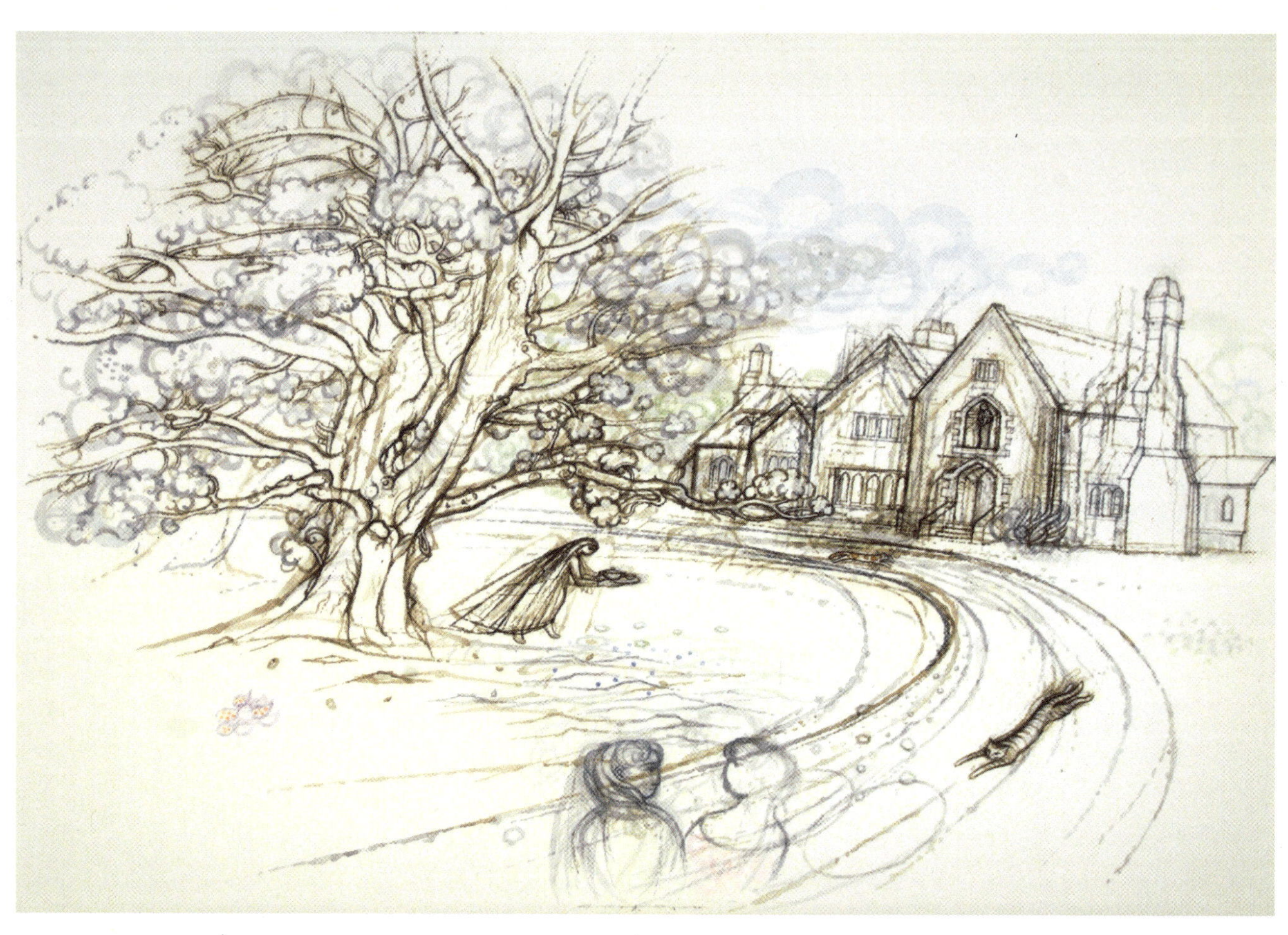

**School garden with a cedar tree**

watercolour

56.5 x 77 cm

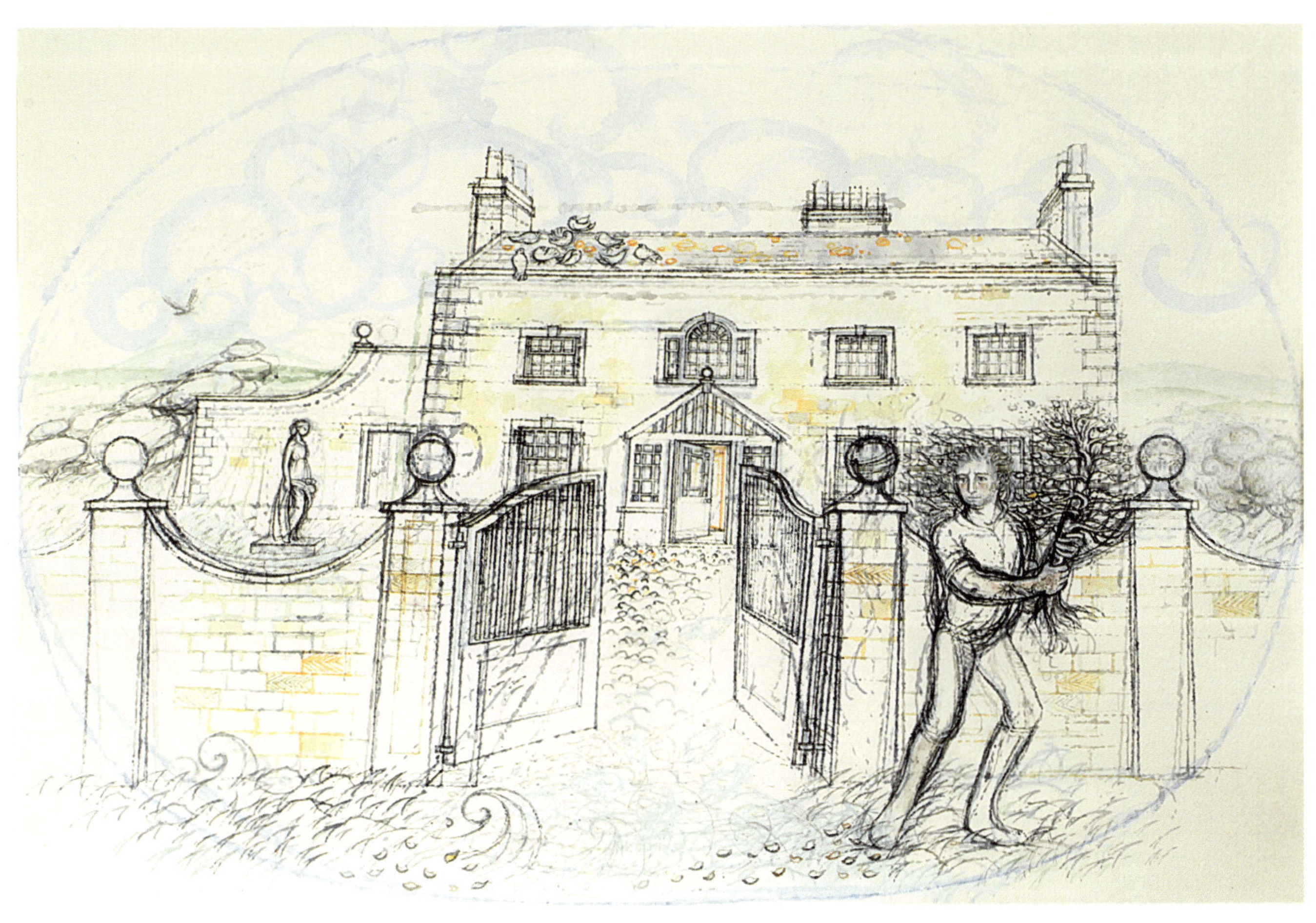

Something foreign and destructive had began in an innocent and beautiful place.

**A man destroying a garden**

brush/watercolour

52 x 76 cm

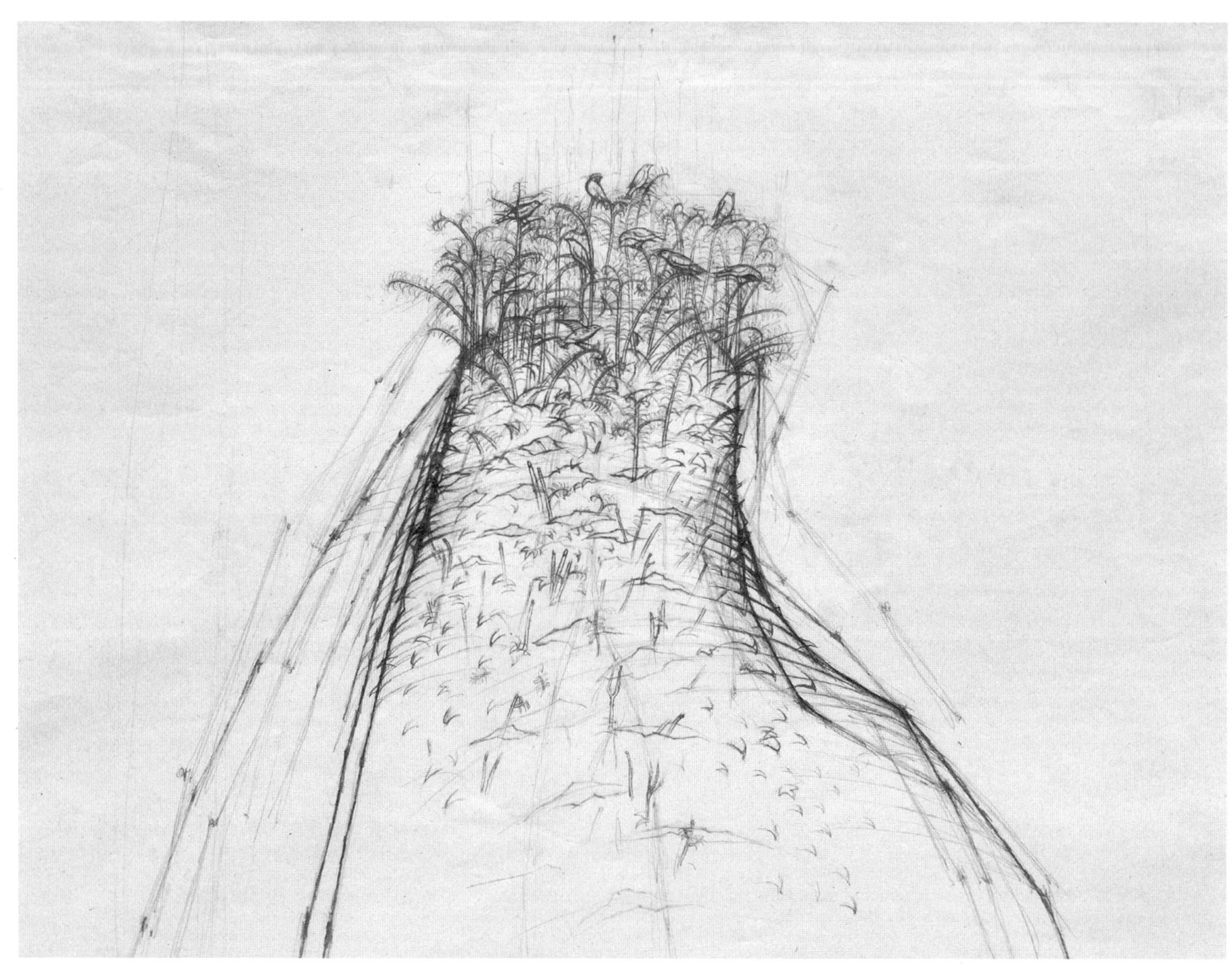

**Tall yew tree by a cottage gate**
(detail) pencil
48 x 62 cm

The tallest of two yew trees at Wykeham that were always alive with the twittering of birds. This one was too high to have the top trimmed.

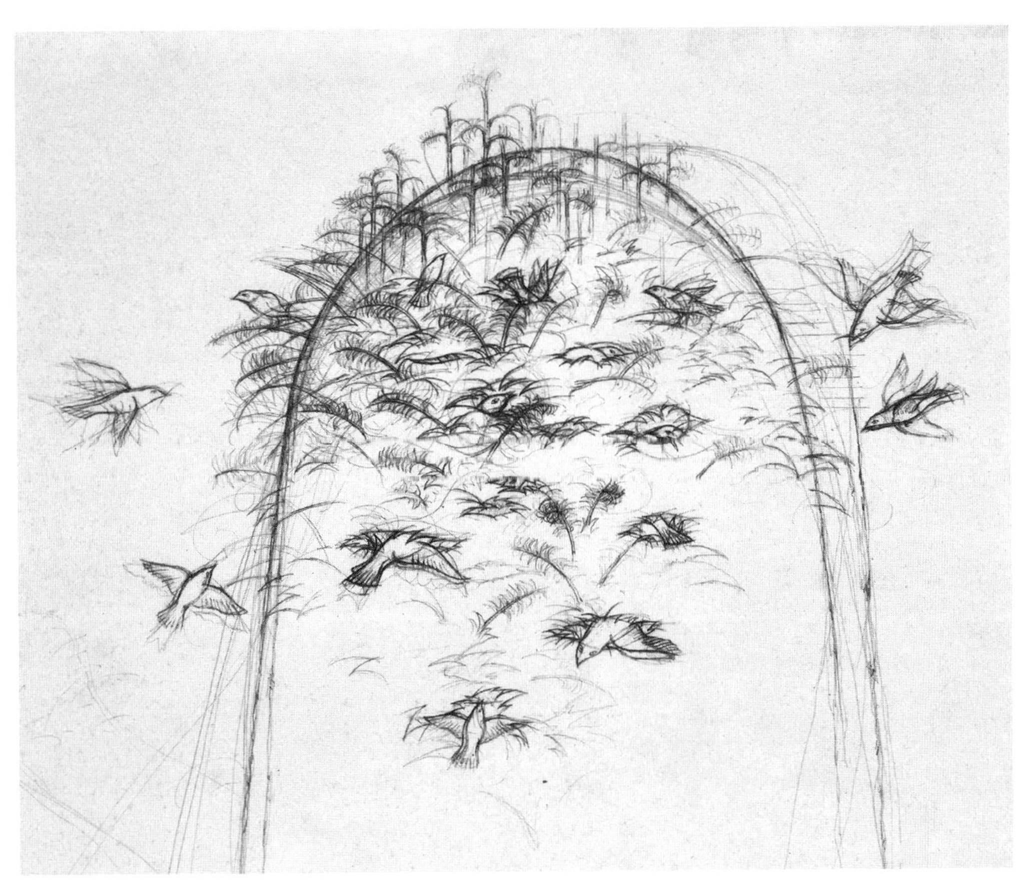

**Yew tree by a cottage gate**

(detail) pencil

38 x 56 cm

# SPEAKING TREES

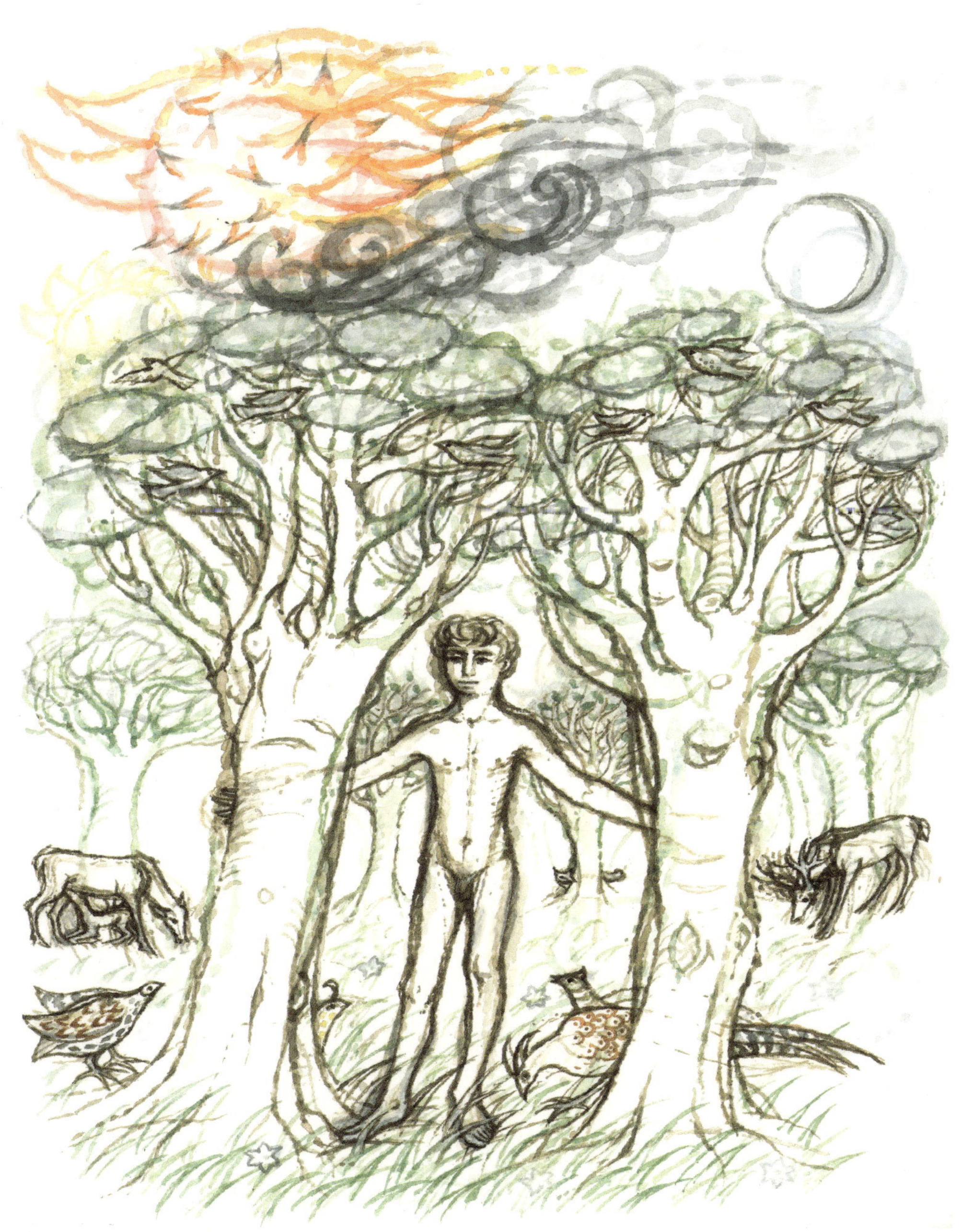

**Protection of Nature:**
trees threatened by global warming
(Resurgence)
brush/watercolour
30.5 x 23 cm

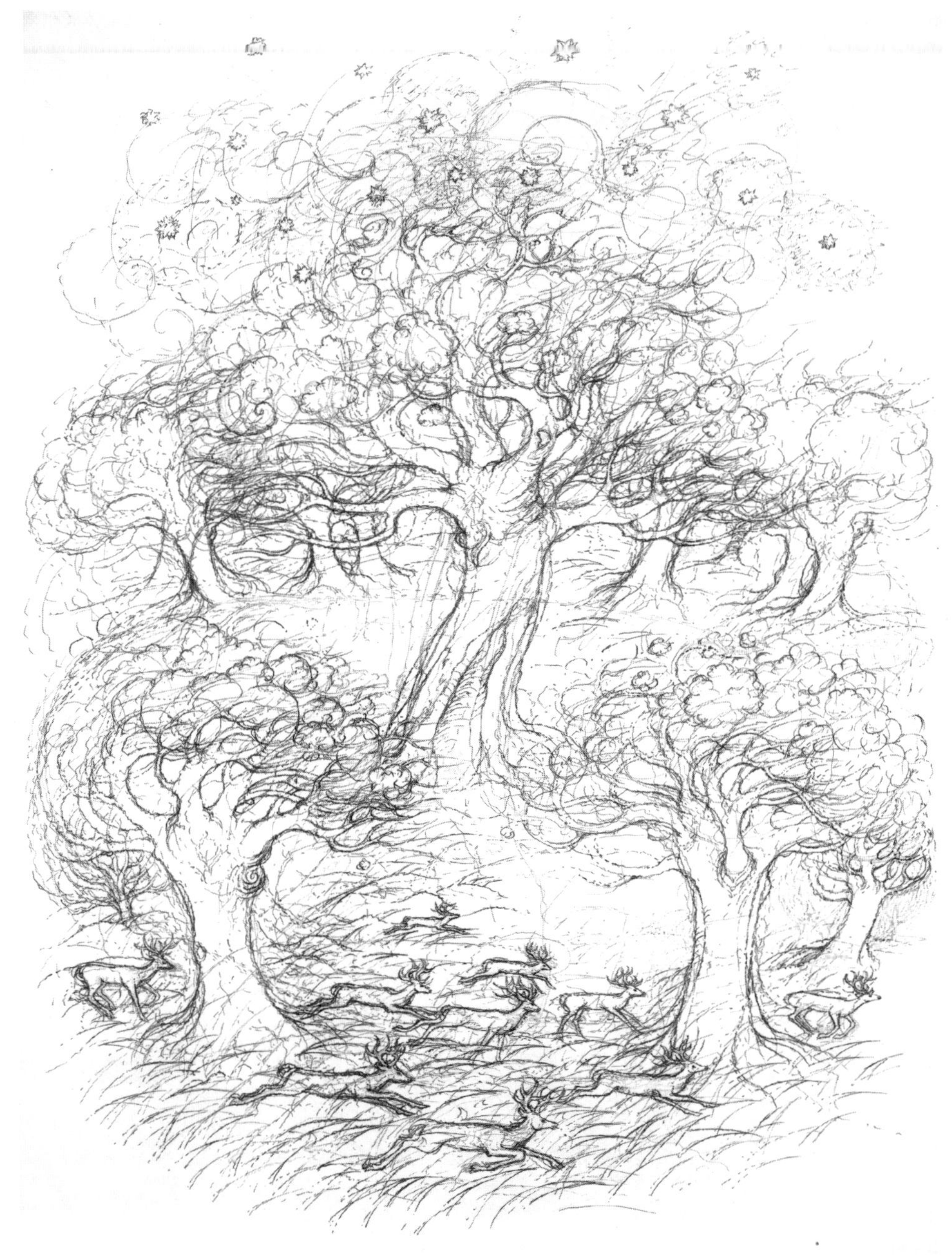

**Stags running at night**
(Resurgence)
indian ink
32 x 45 cm

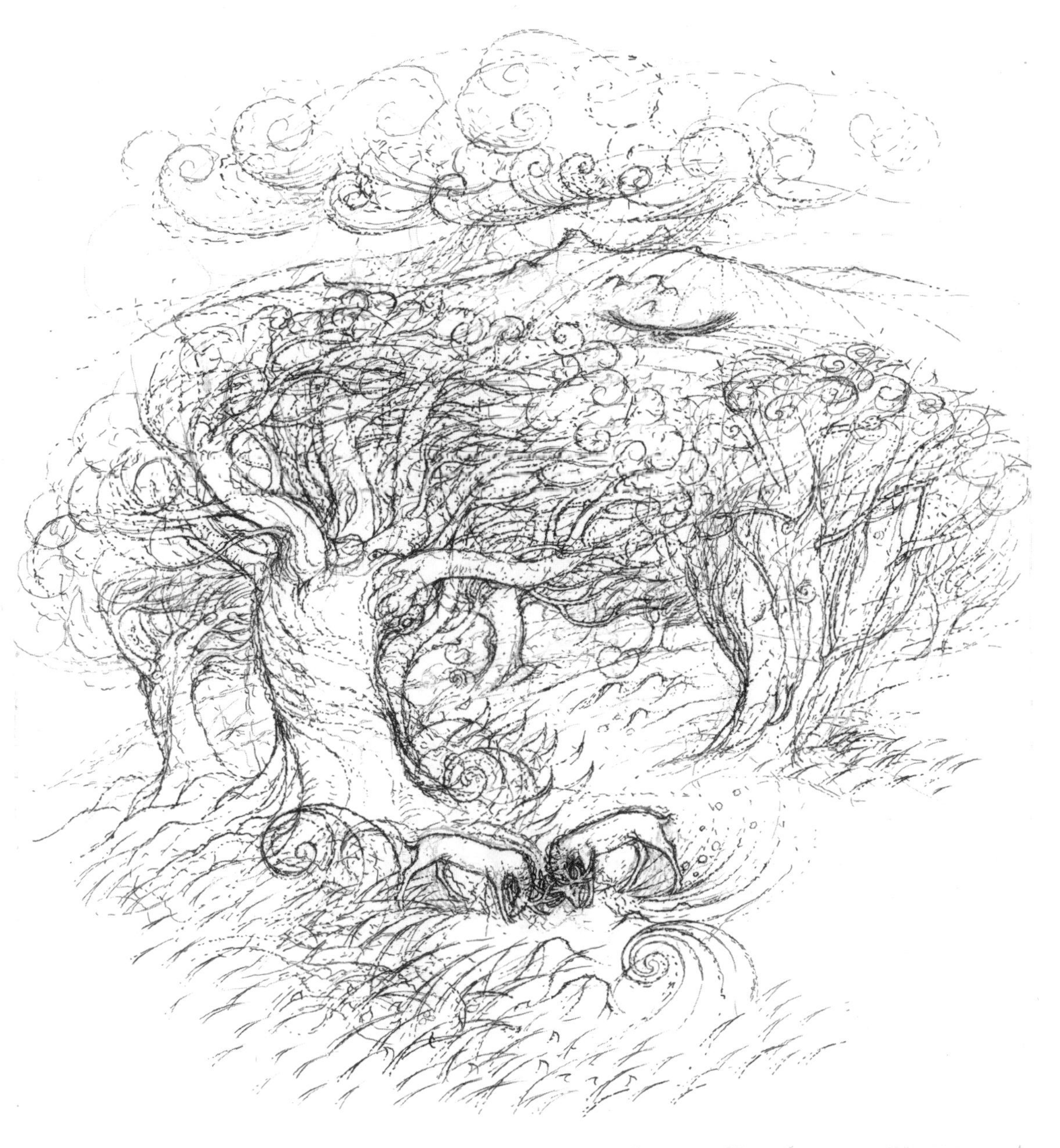

**Wilderness I:**
stags fighting
indian ink
41.5 x 32 cm

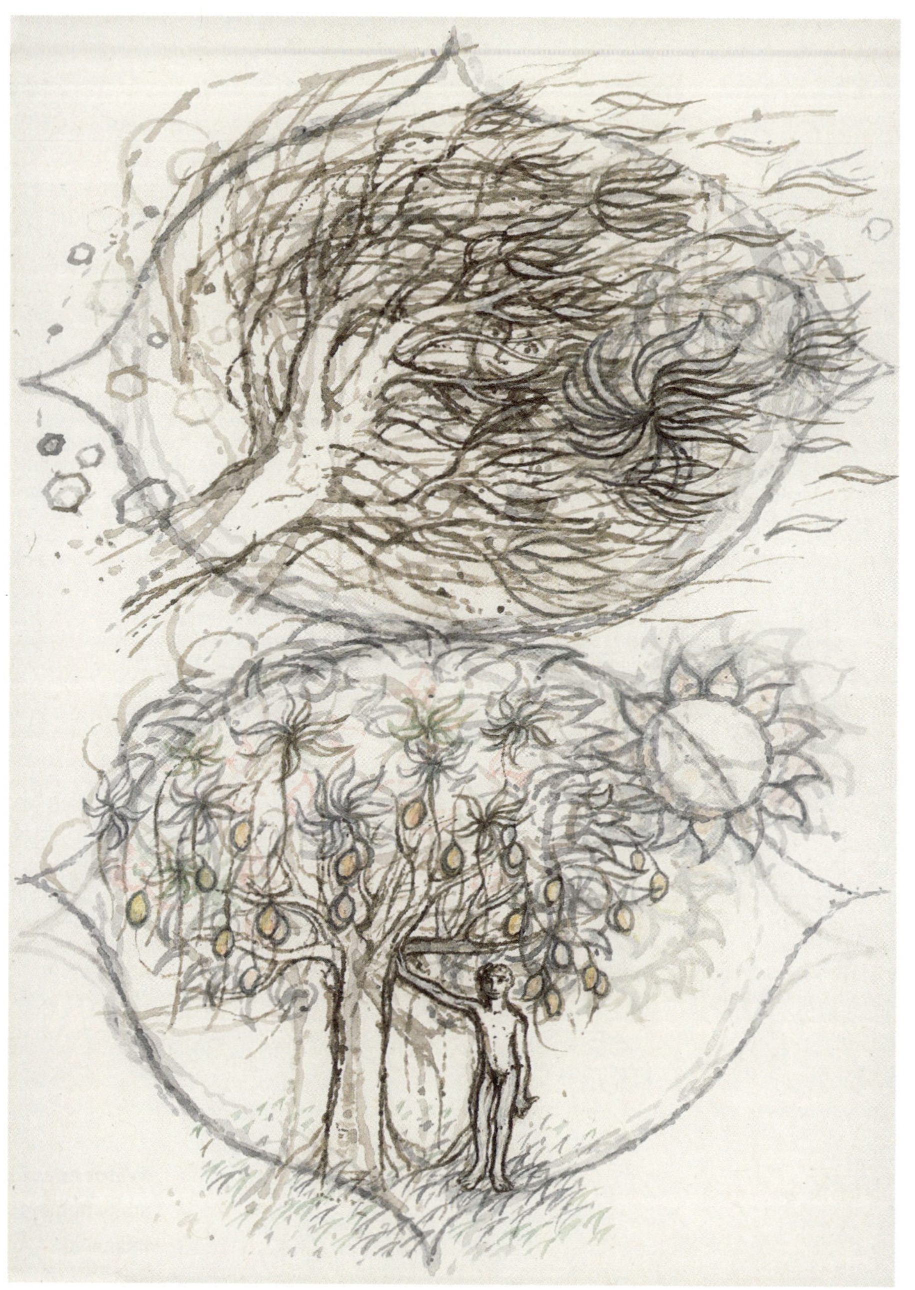

This tree, brought down in a heavy storm, was saved and rescued by friends. It continues to give abundant fruit.

**The god of the Mango Tree**
(Resurgence)
brush/watercolour
41.5 x 32 cm

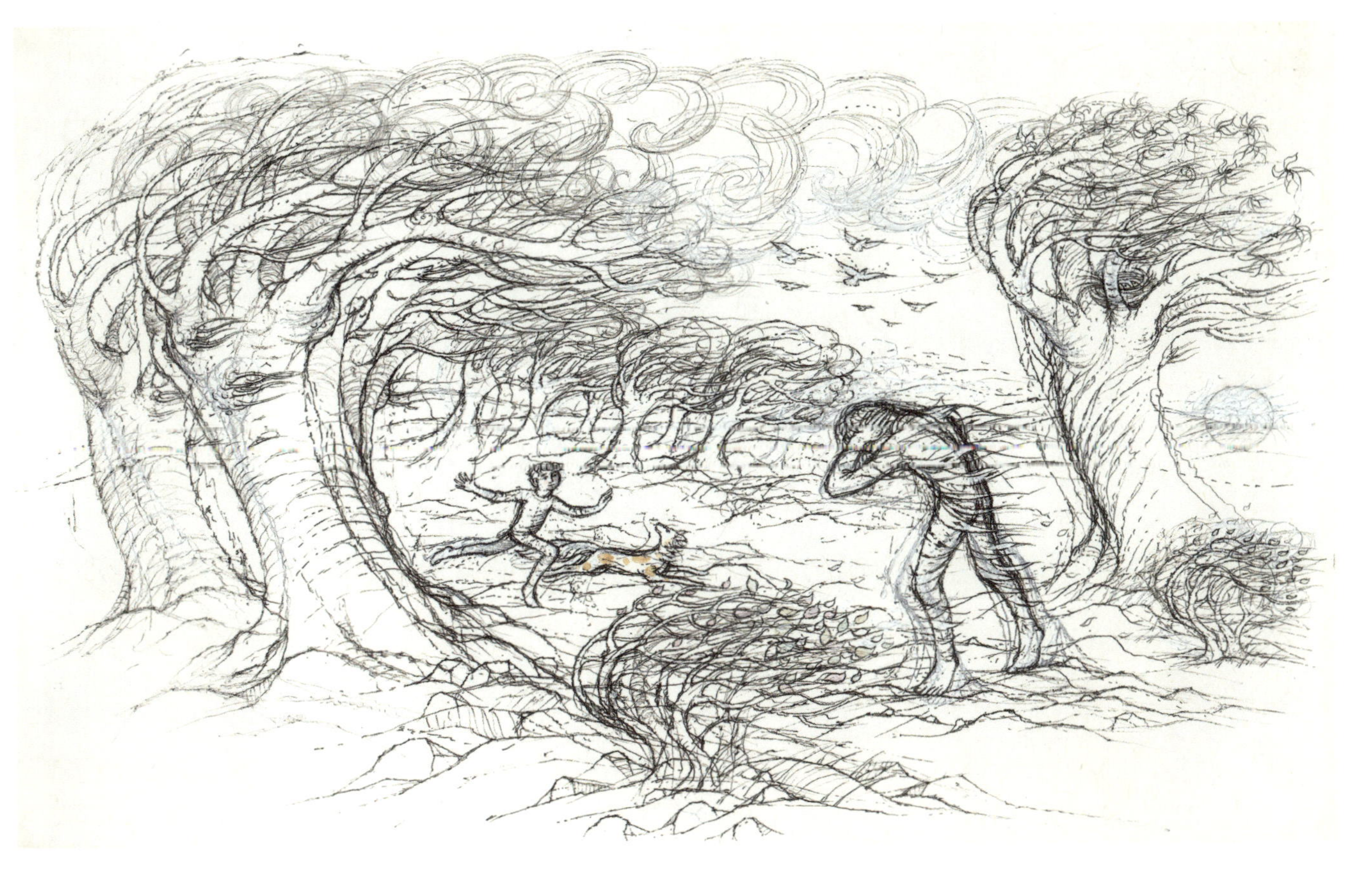

Inspired by William Blake's "Songs of Innocence".

**Wilderness II:**
the lost child
indian ink
37 x 56 cm

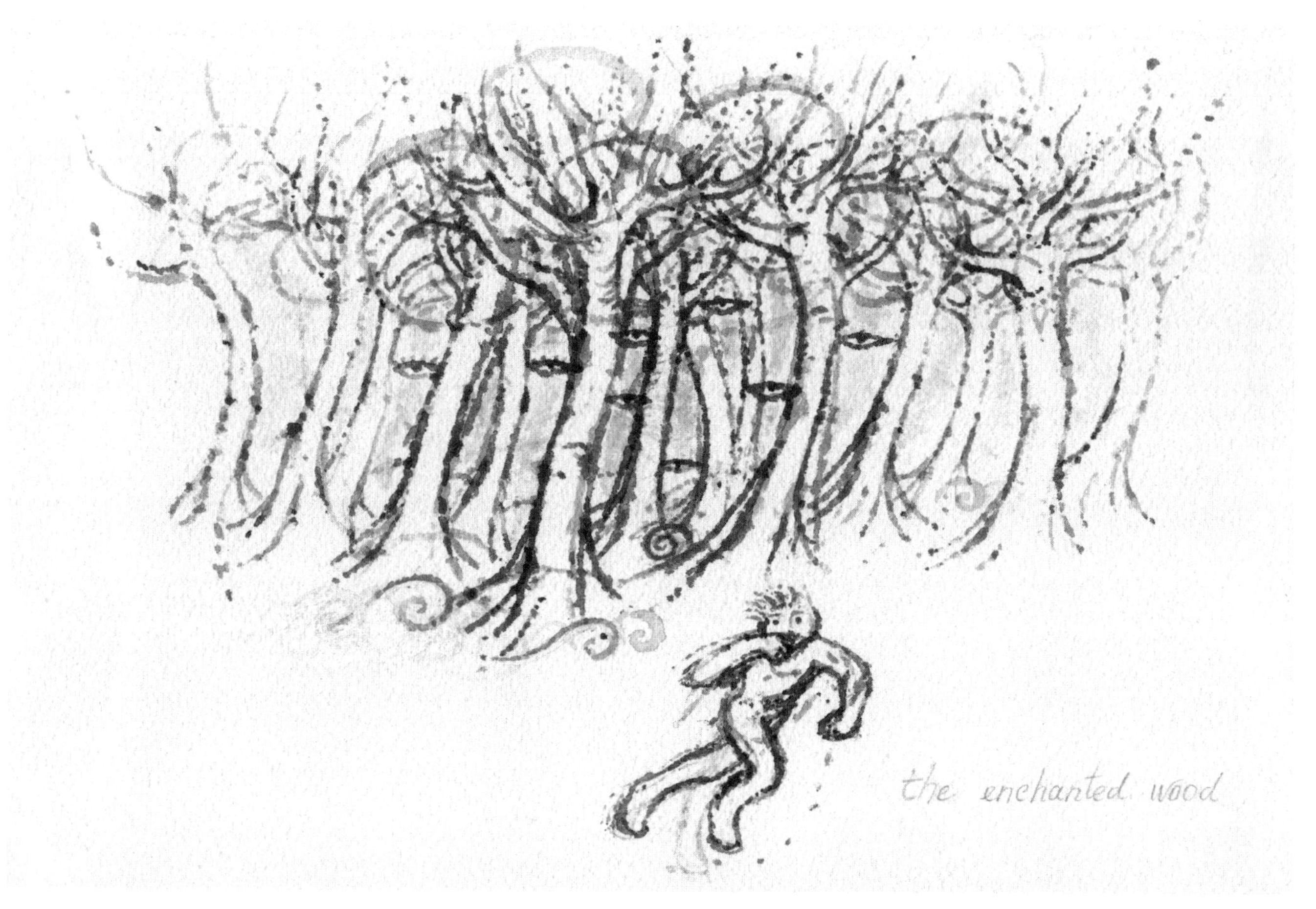


**The enchanted wood**

brush/watercolour

19.5 x 32 cm

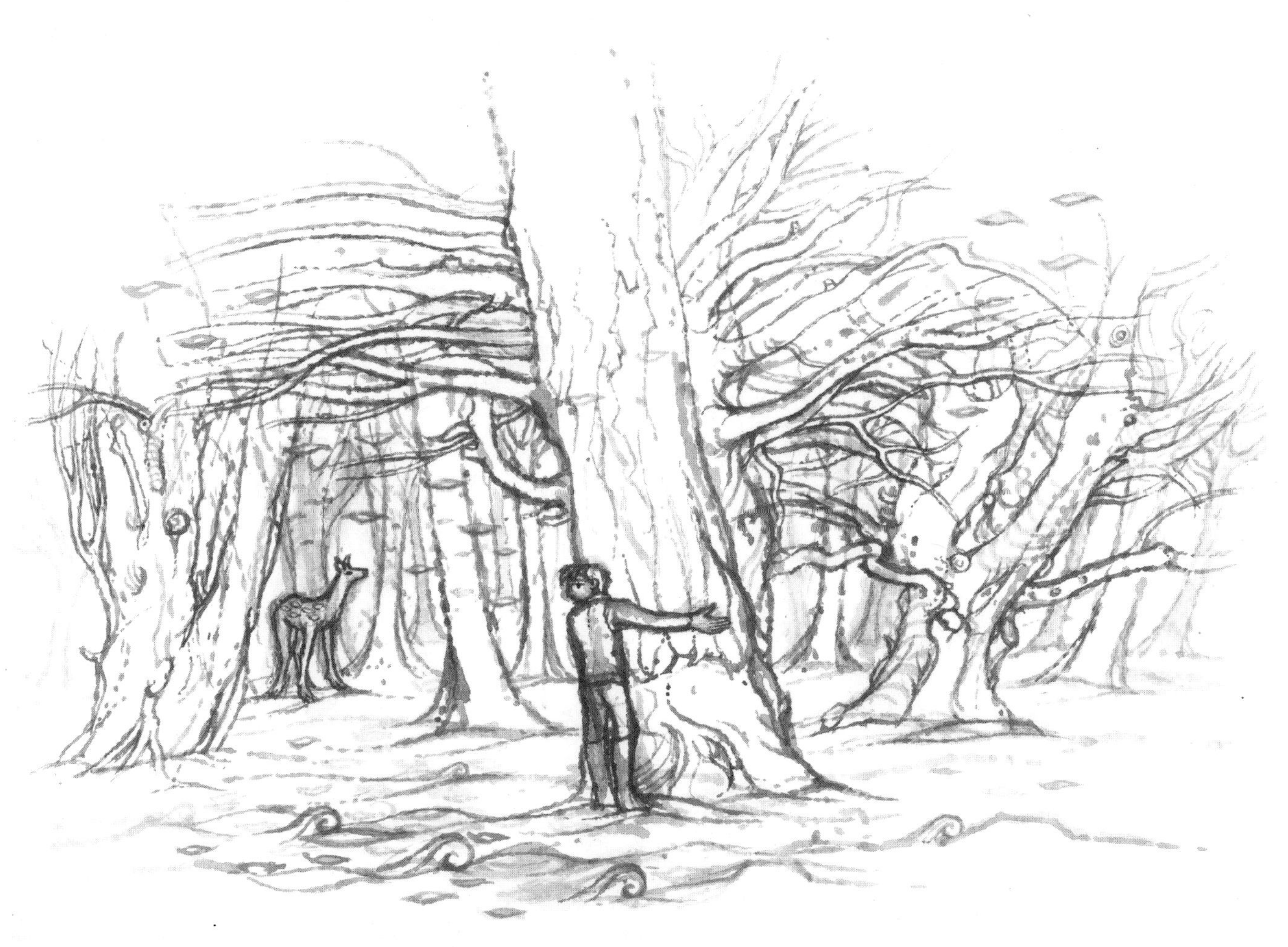

**A man startled by a strange animal**
(Resurgence)
watercolour
23 x 31 cm

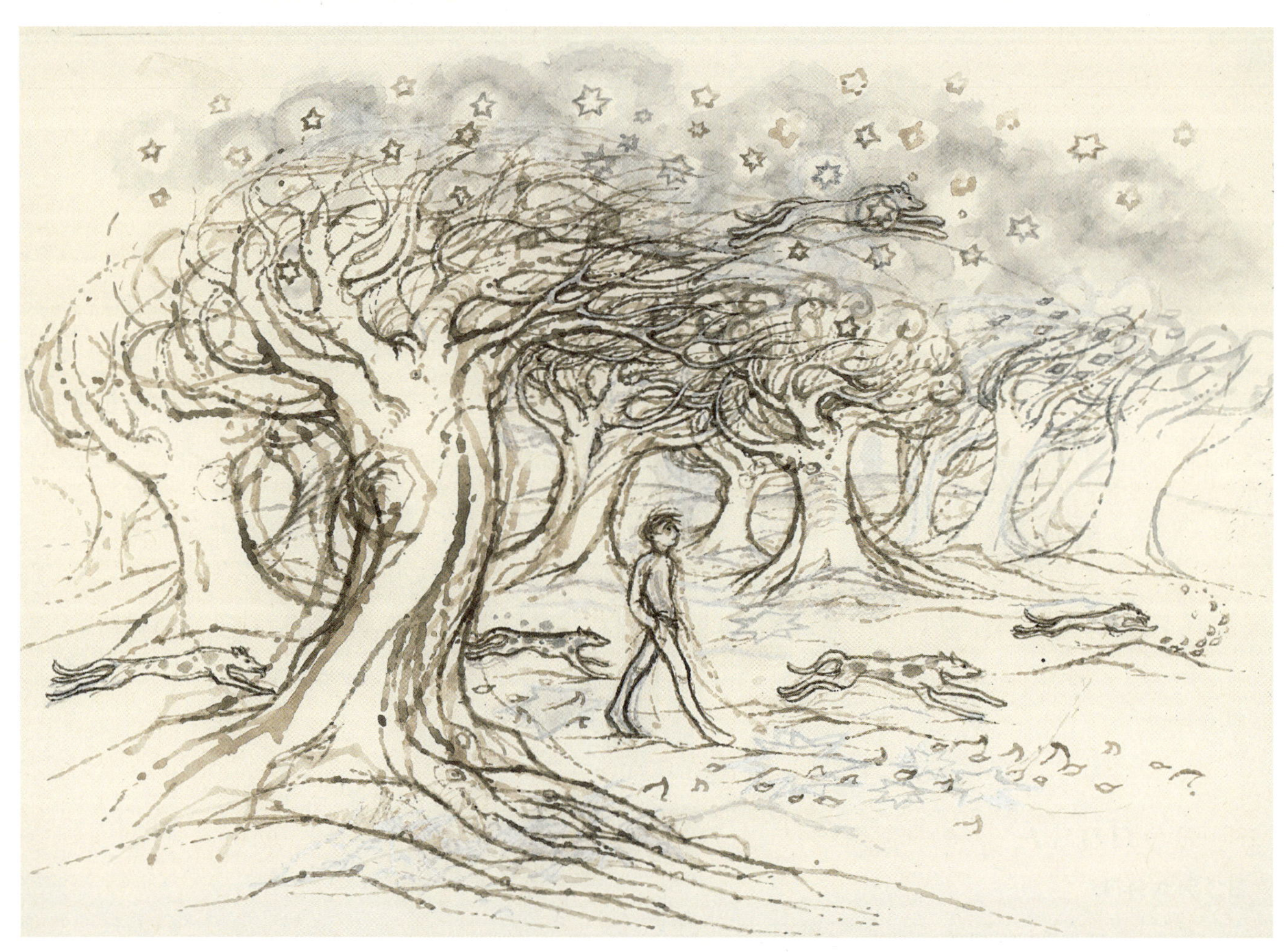

**Dog days and Dog nights**

brush/watercolour

28 x 37.5 cm

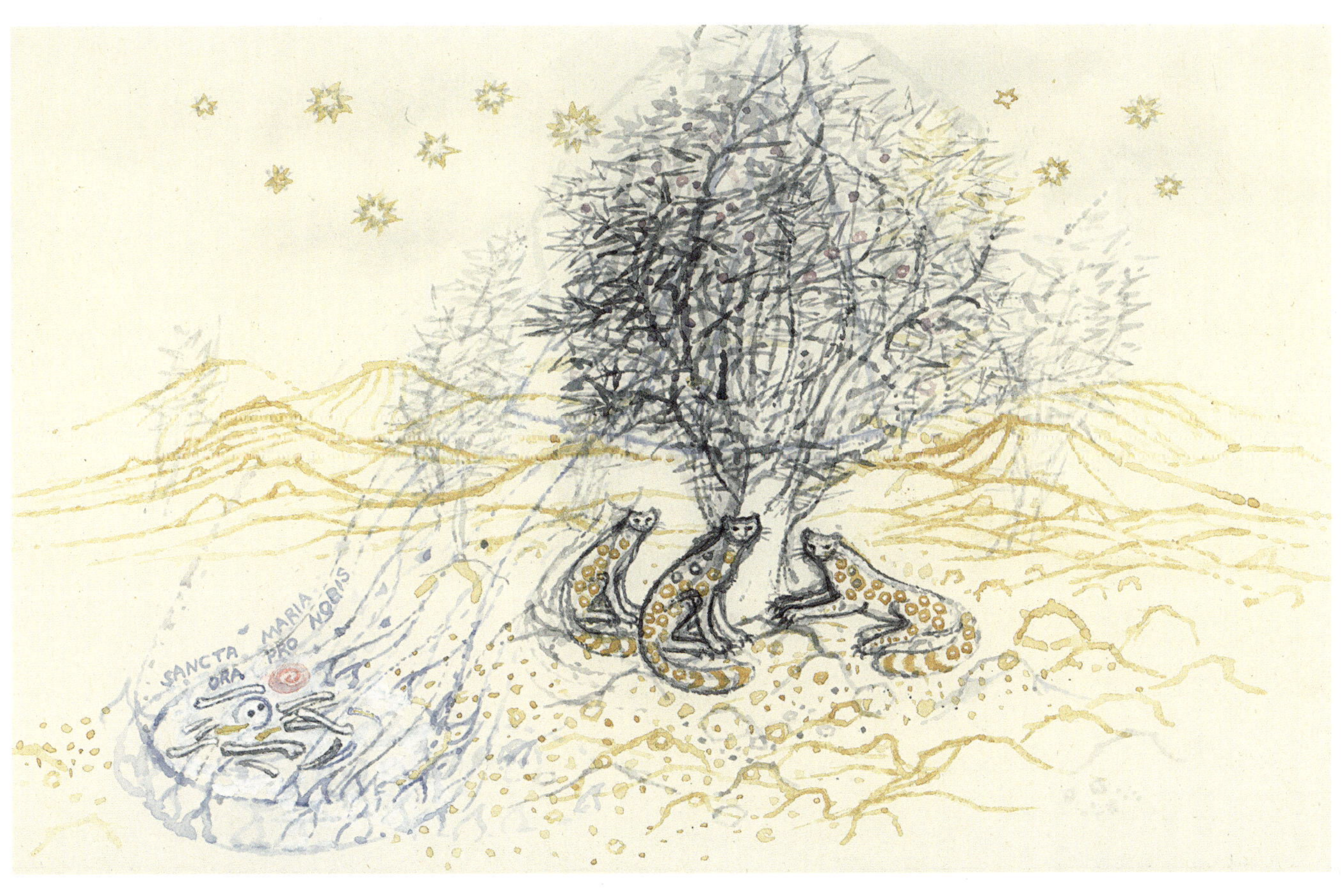


Inspired by T.S. Eliot's poem "Ash Wednesday";
"Lady, three white leopards sat under a juniper tree
In the cool of the day ......"

**Ash Wednesday**
watercolour
22 x 35 cm

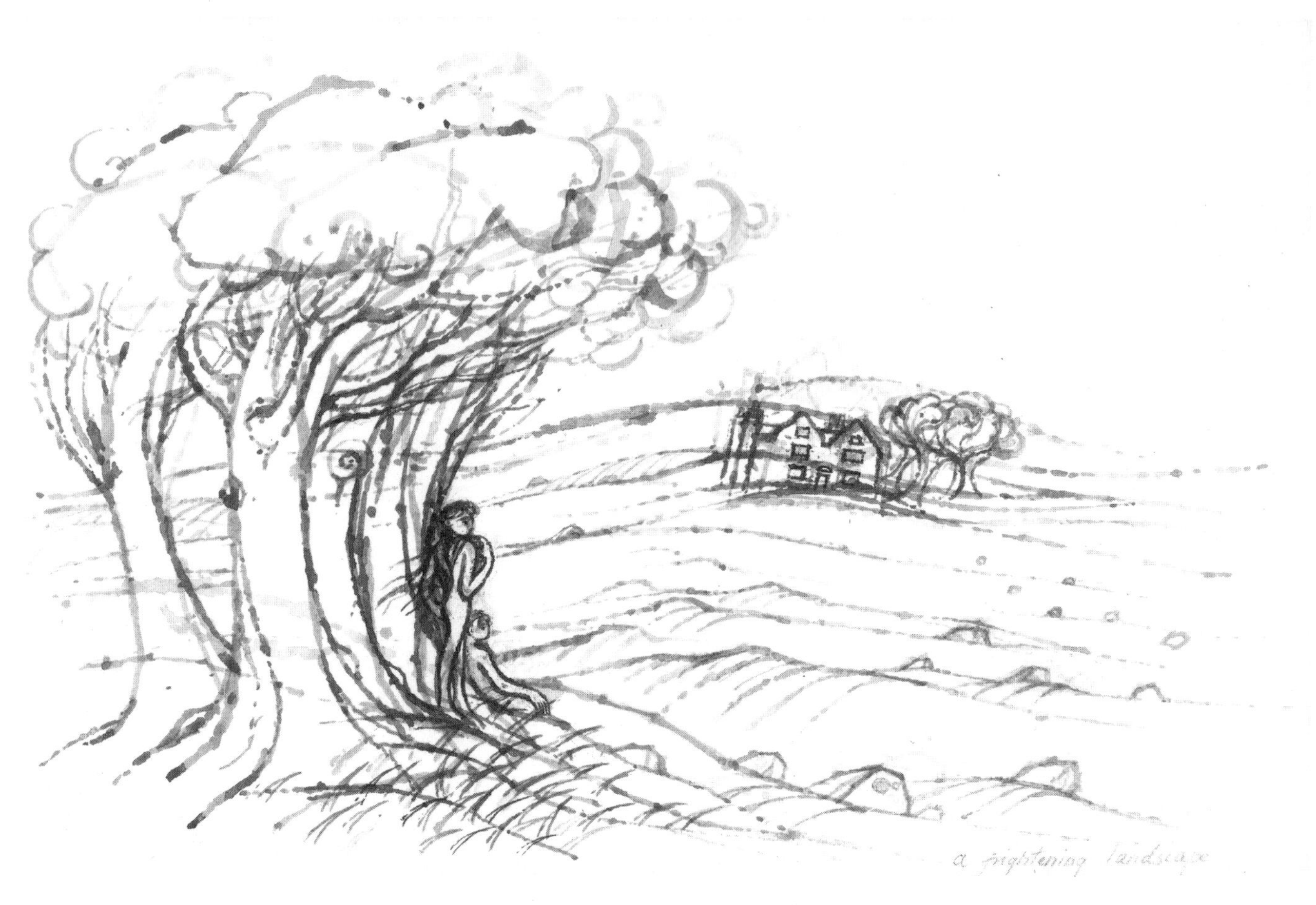


**People guarding a house**

watercolour

19.5 x 28.5

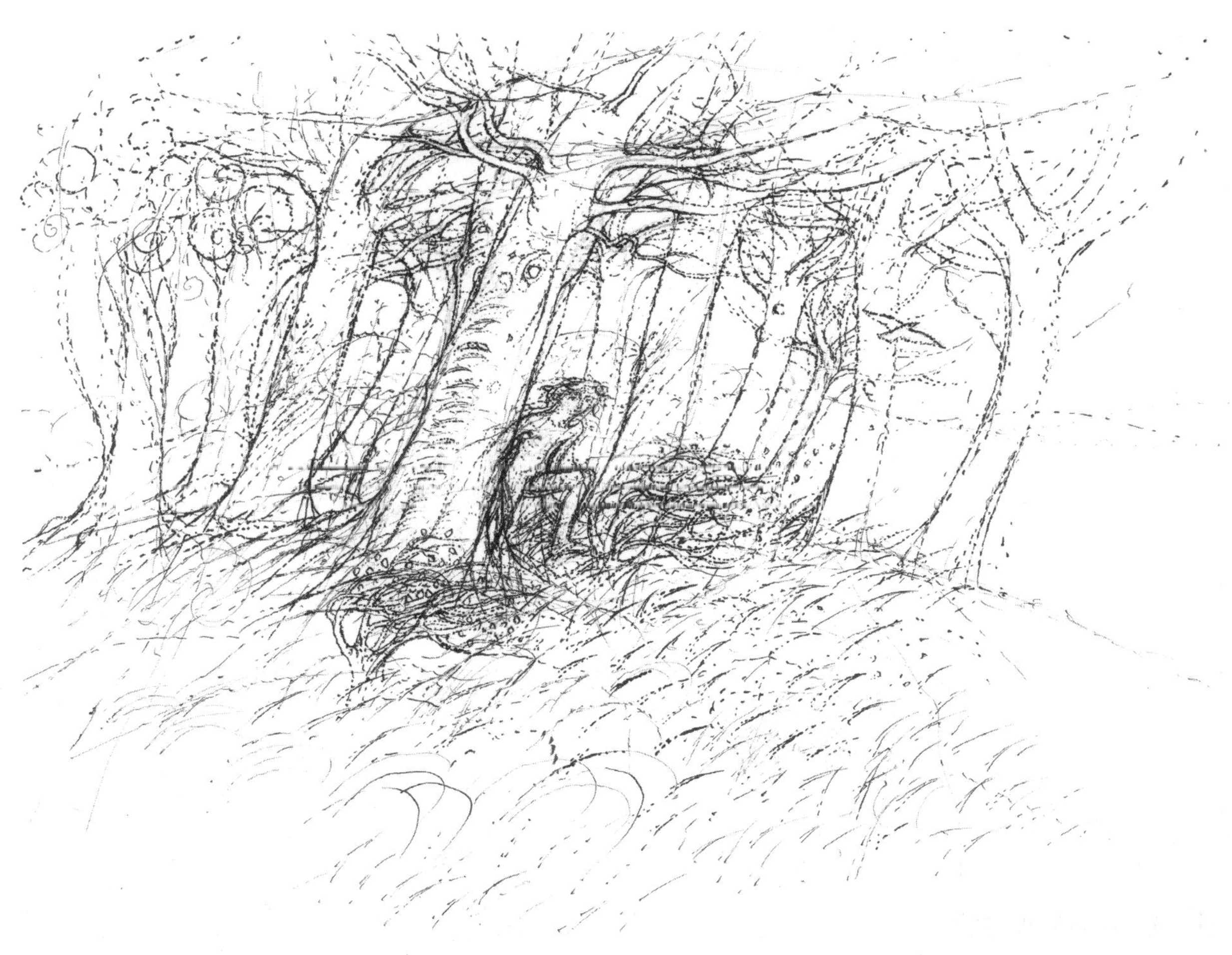

**The wild boy**
indian ink
31 x 41 cm

# LIFE IN NATURE

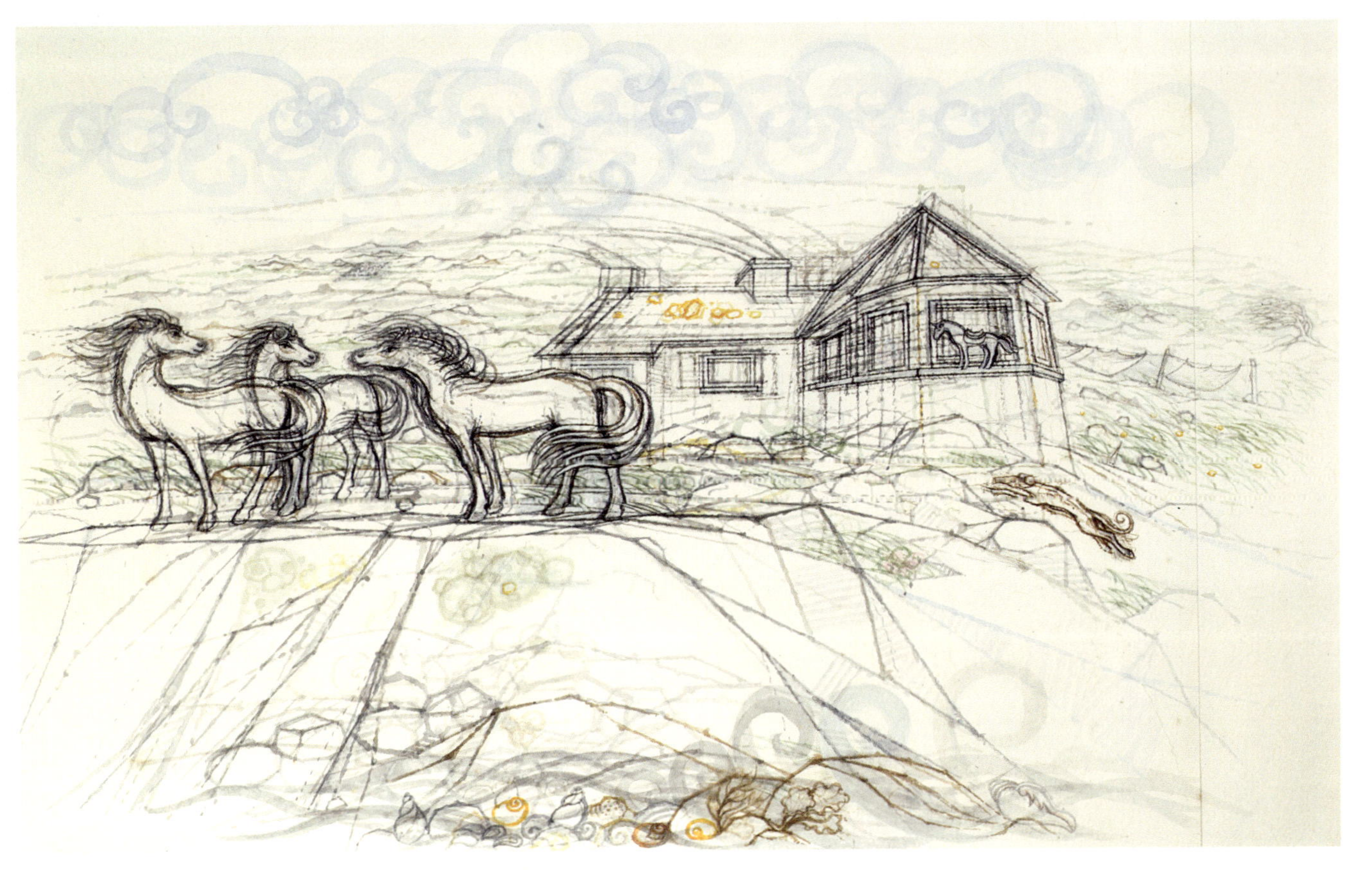

White horses stand together on a rocky platform above the sea.

**Connemara, Ireland**

brush/watercolour

56 x 87 cm

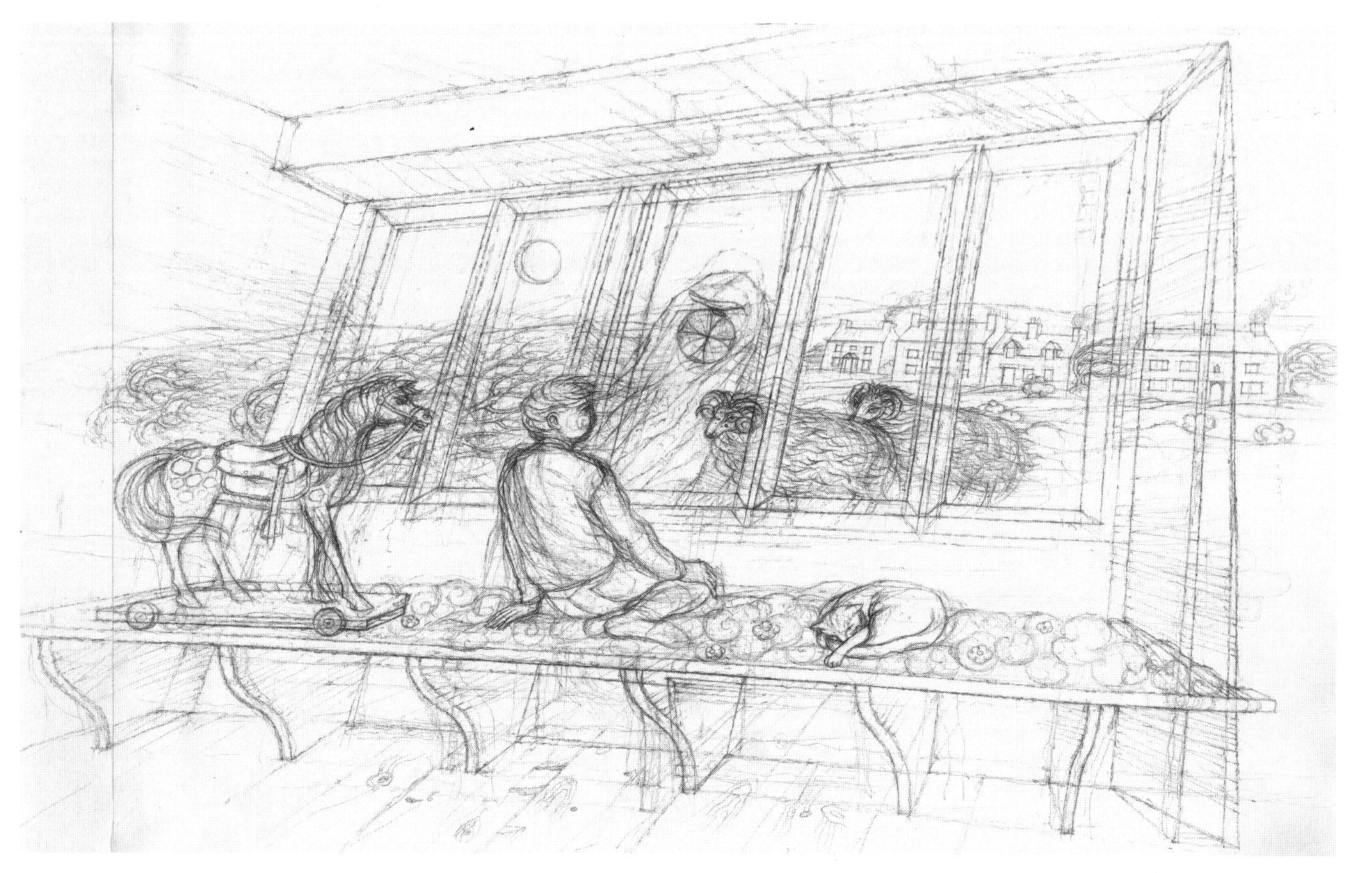

**The window seat:**
a farm on the North Yorkshire Moors
pencil
42 x 67 cm

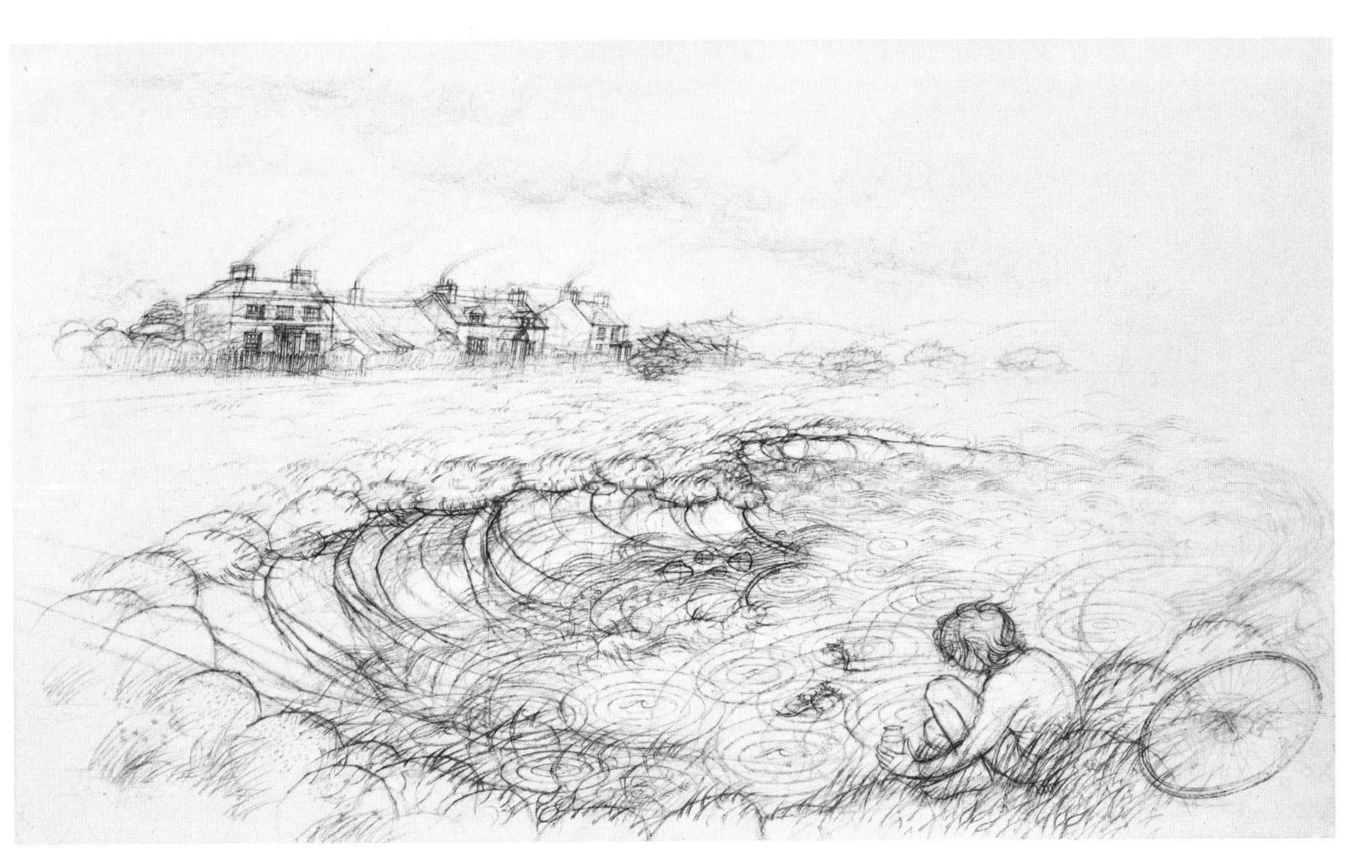

**A pond high on a common:**
a child fishes for newts
pencil
52 x 78 cm

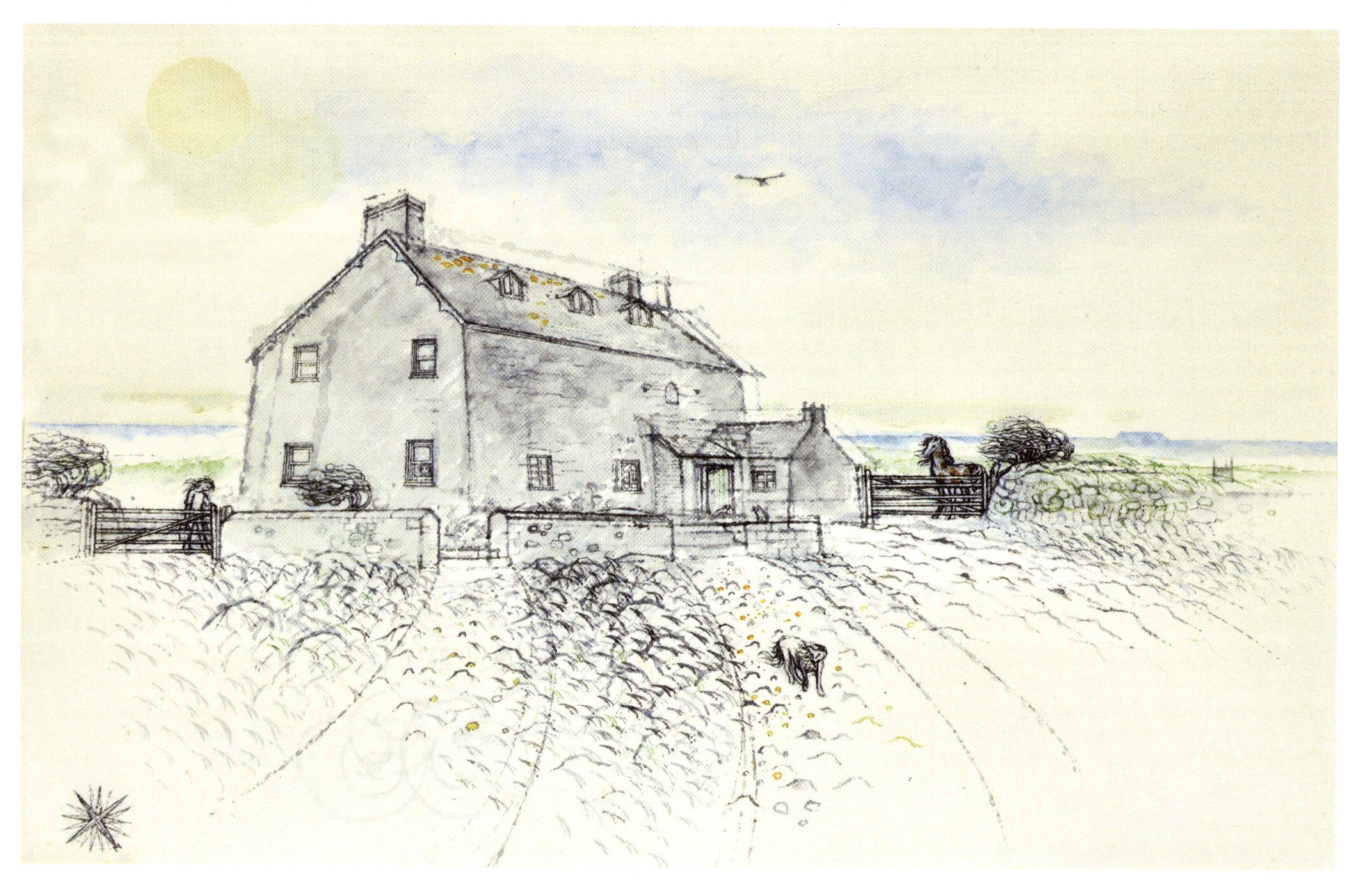

**Little Barton, North Devon**
watercolour
56.5 x 76 cm

"North Devon Light" was the theme of an Exhibition at the Plough Gallery, Great Torrington.

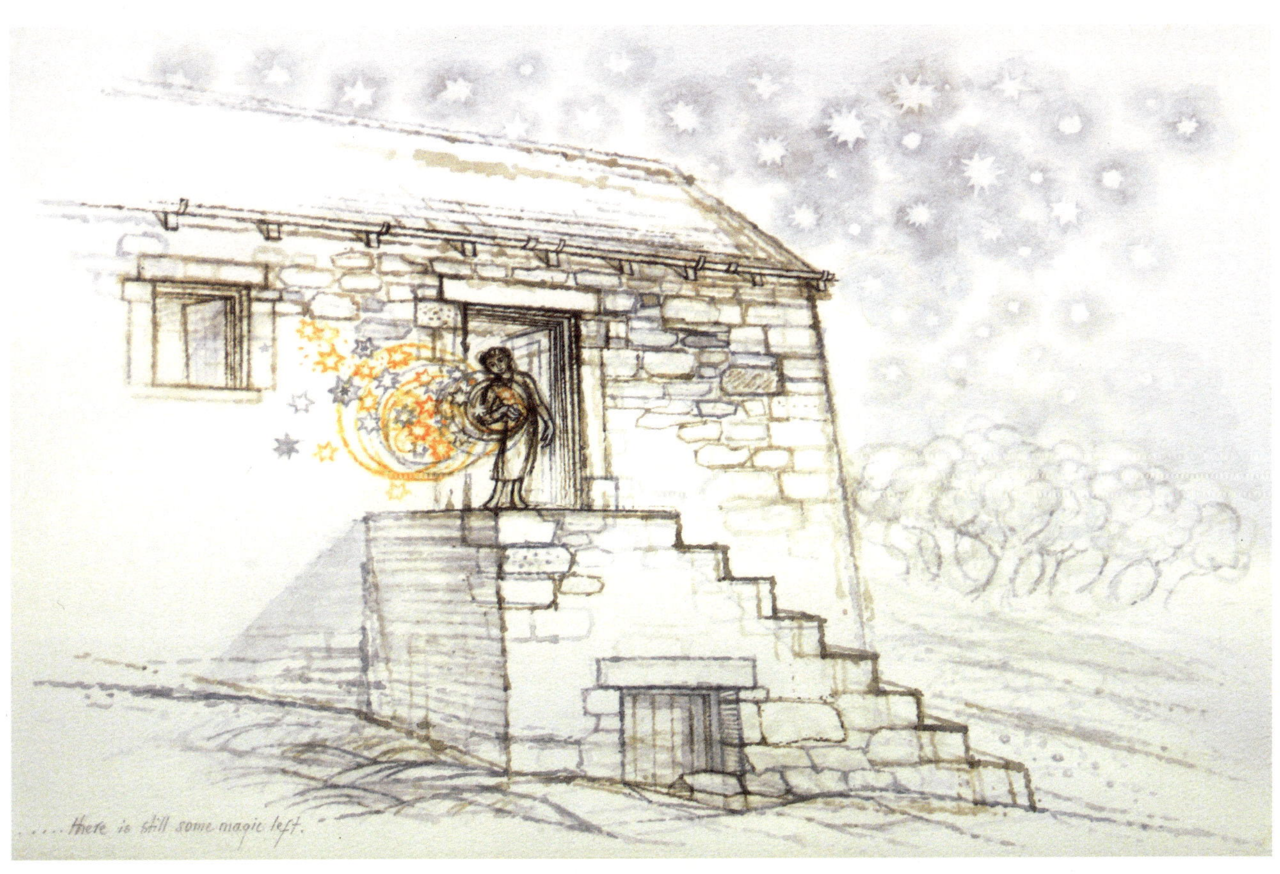


While out for a walk in gathering darkness, a boy suddenly popped out of a farm building and waved a sparkler around. My companion remarked that "there is still some magic left."

**There is still Magic left ...**

watercolour

38.5 x 56 cm

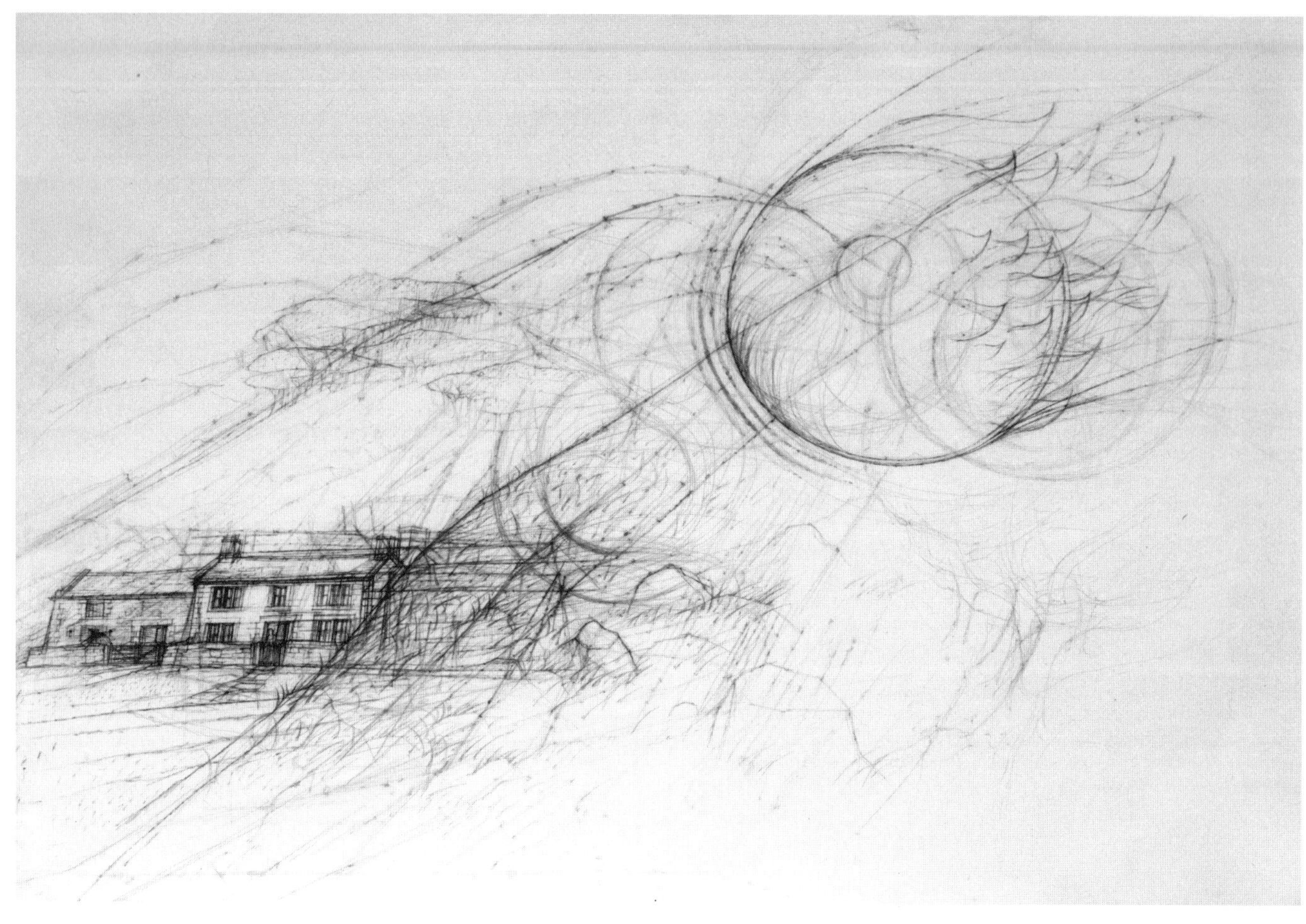

**Farmhouse and Sun**

pencil

53 x 76 cm

As we stopped to buy eggs at a Derbyshire farm, the woman of the house excitedly announced that the sun was about to appear round the hill for a brief few minutes, the only time during the day that it could be seen.

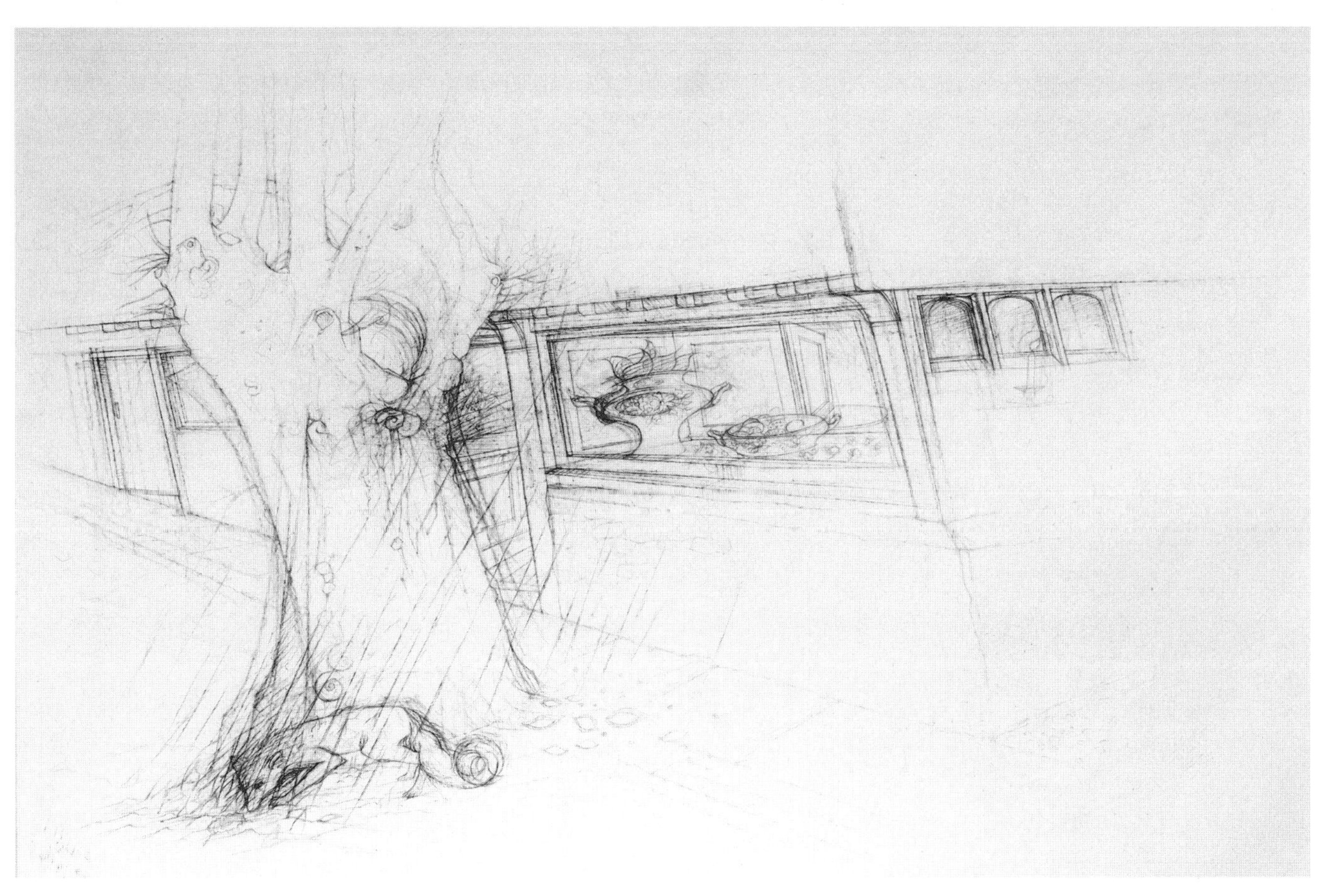

**The Town Tree**
pencil
57 x 82 cm

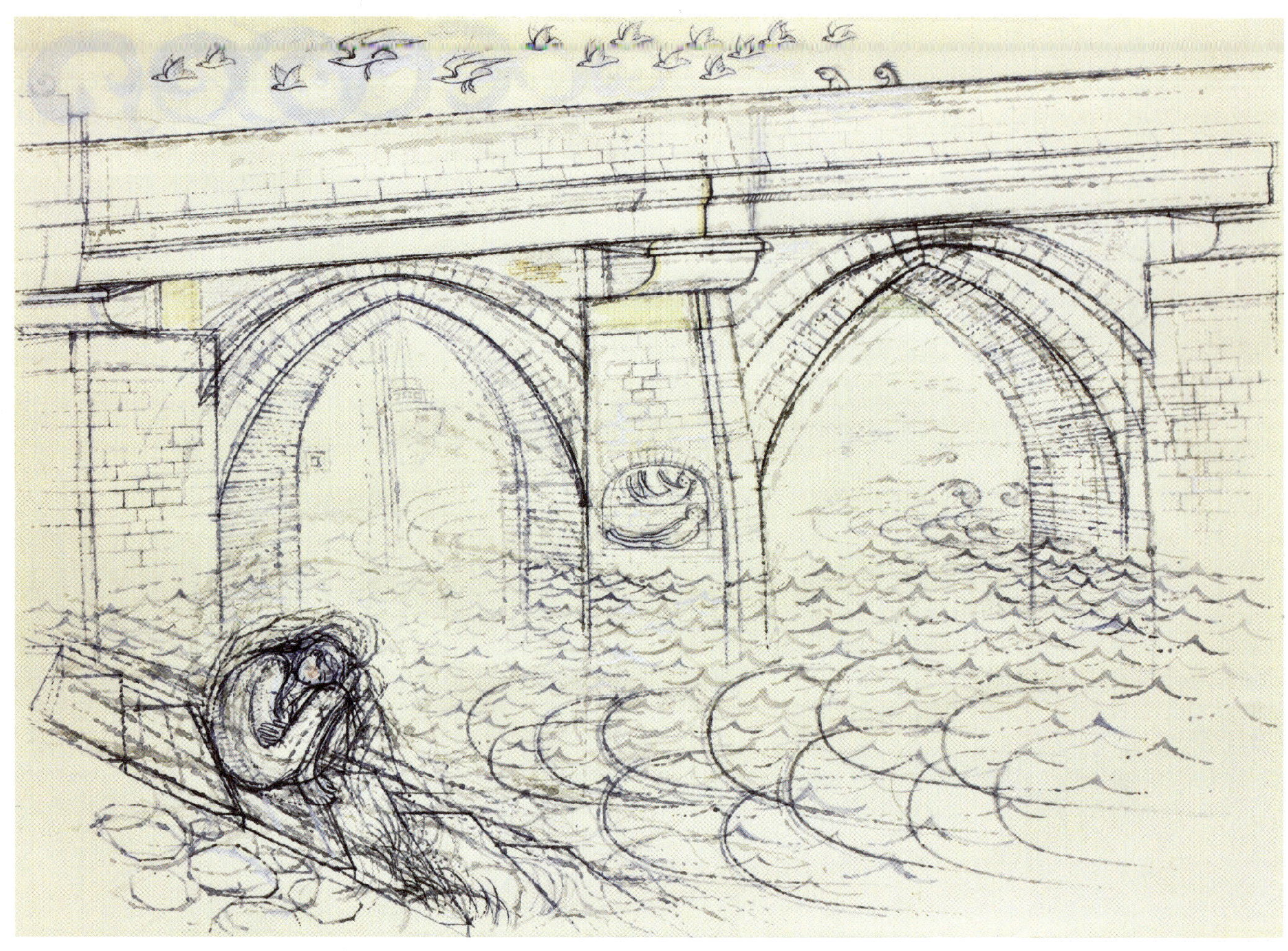

**Bideford Bridge**

watercolour

57 x 76 cm

“The Bridges of North Devon” was the subject of an exhibition at the Plough in Torrington.

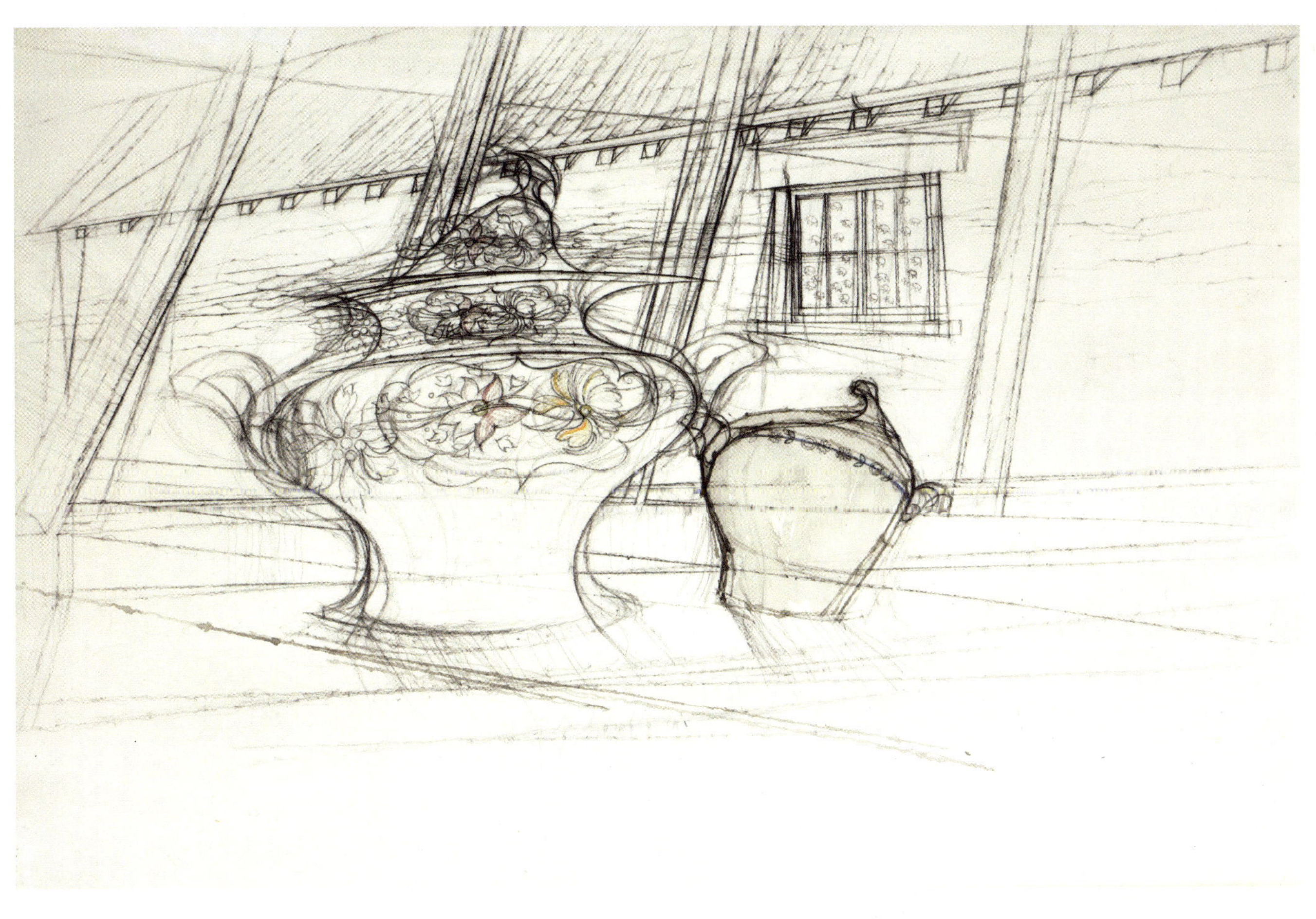

**Pots on a windowsill**
pencil and watercolour
51 x 75 cm

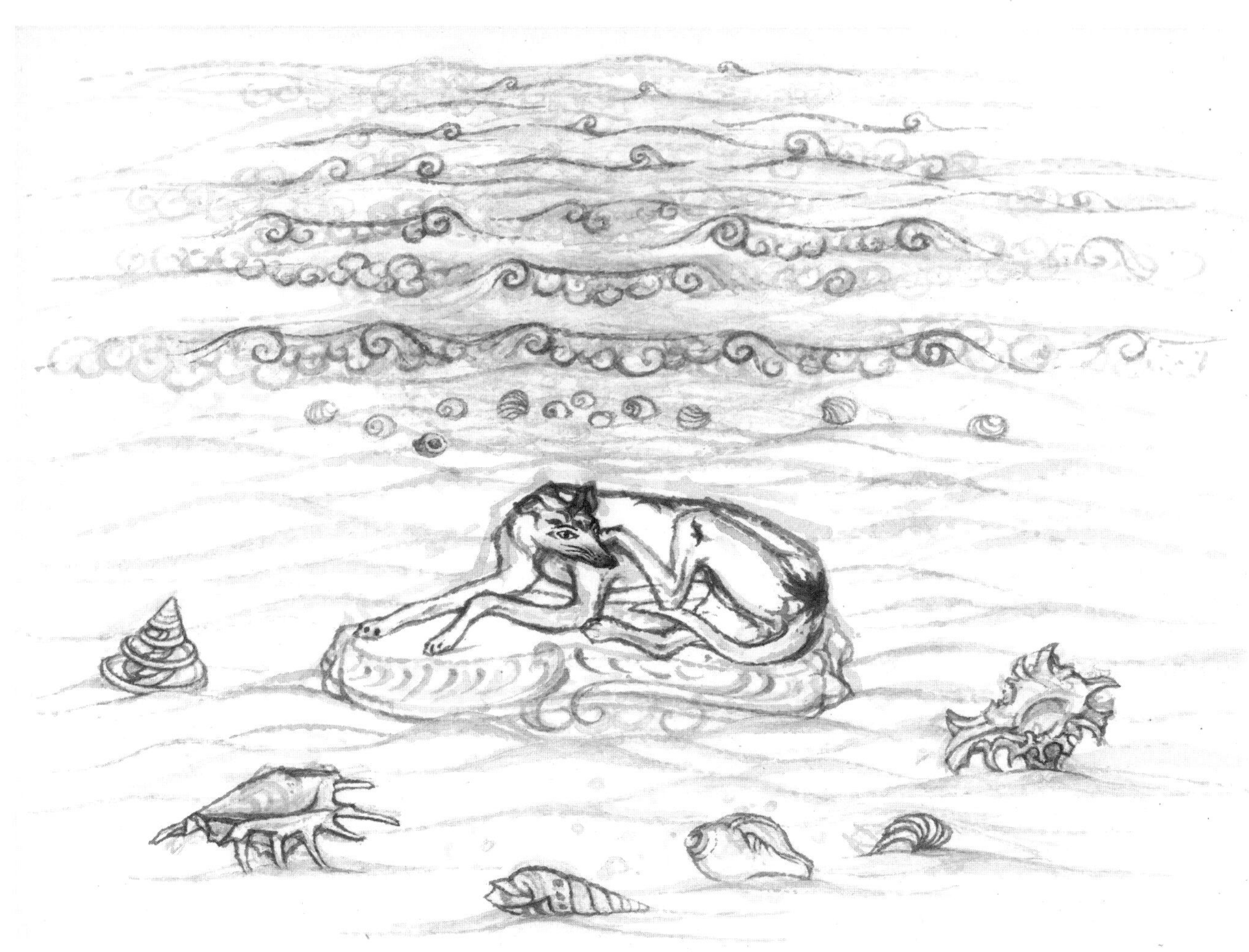

**China dog by the sea**

watercolour

29.5 x 39 cm

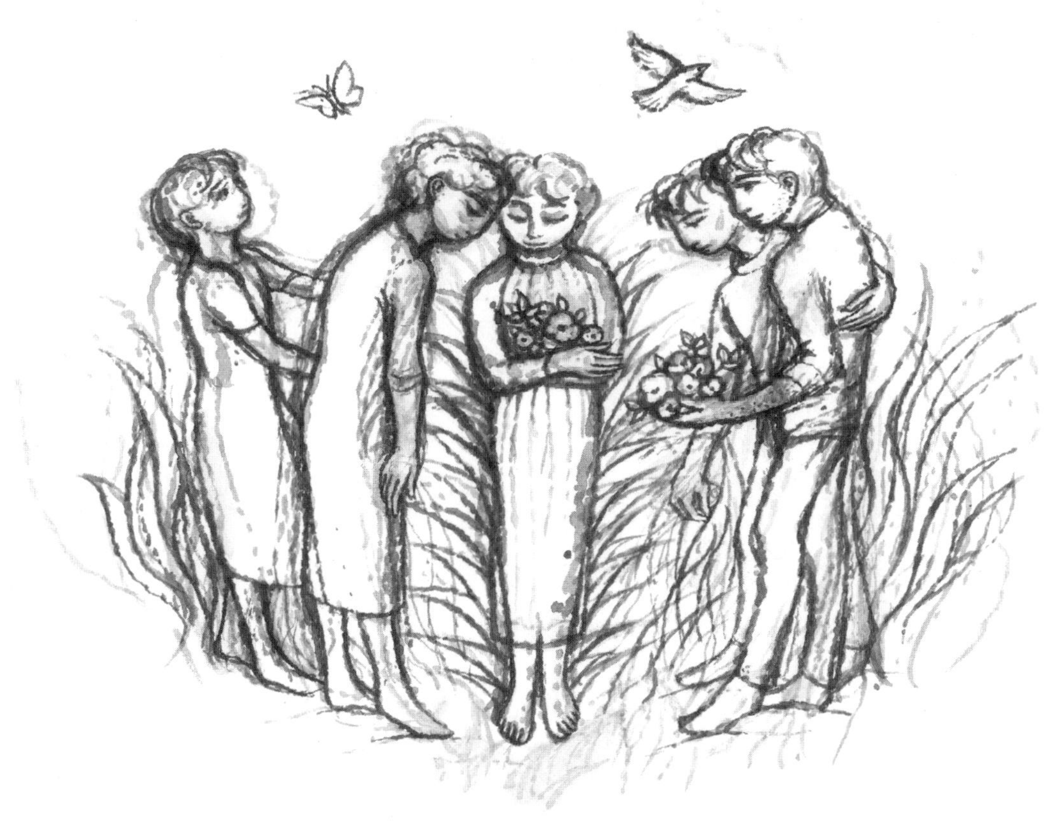

**A good death**
(Resurgence)
watercolour
23 x 30.5 cm

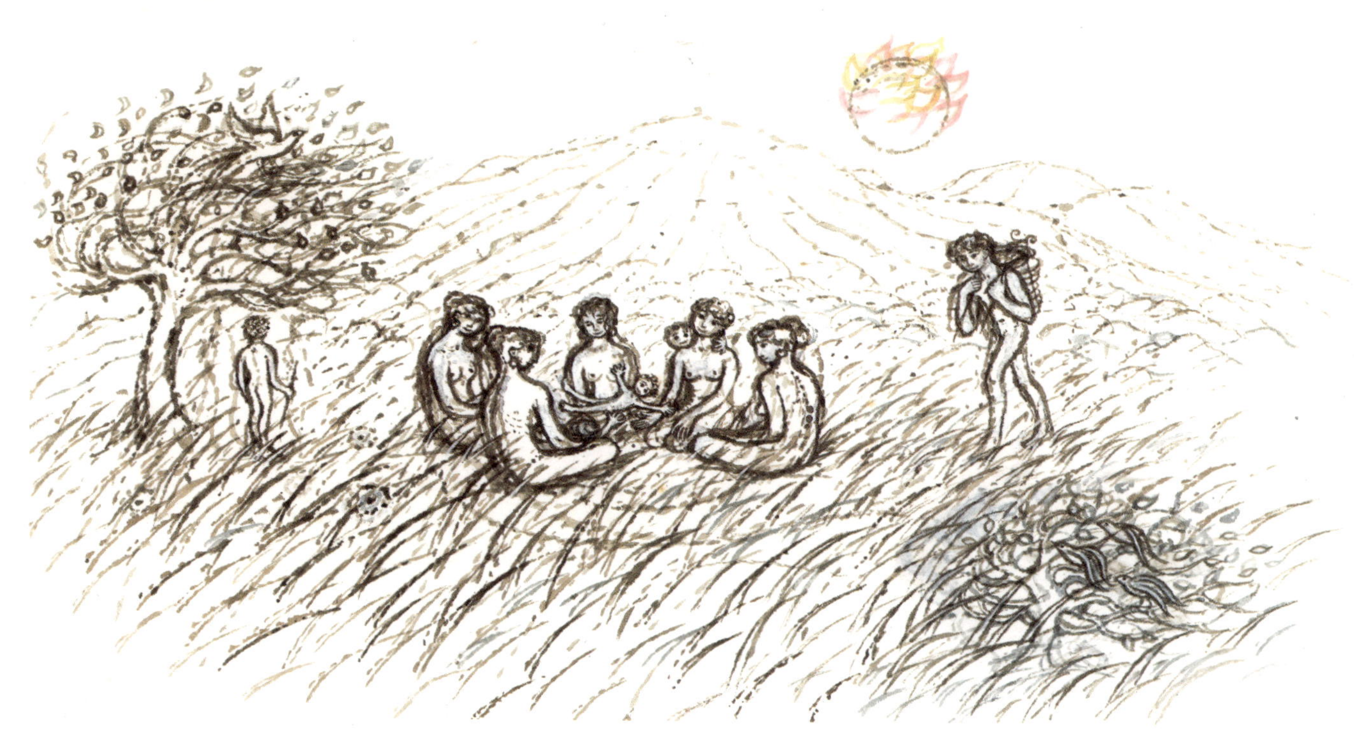

**A good education**

(Resurgence)

watercolour

26 x 38 cm

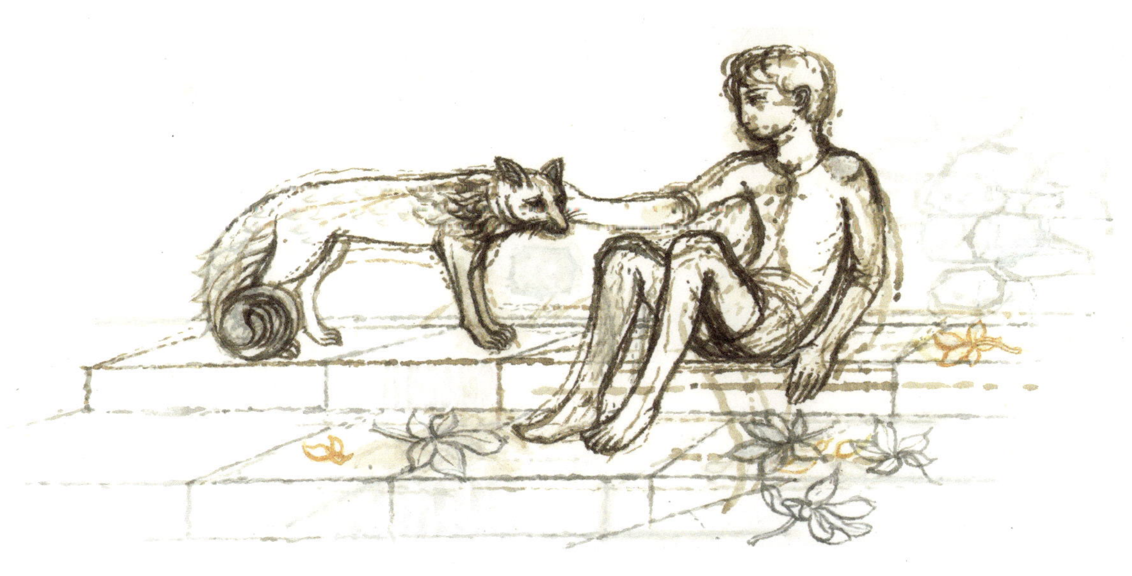

**A poor boy with a pet fox**
brush/watercolour
17 x 44 cm

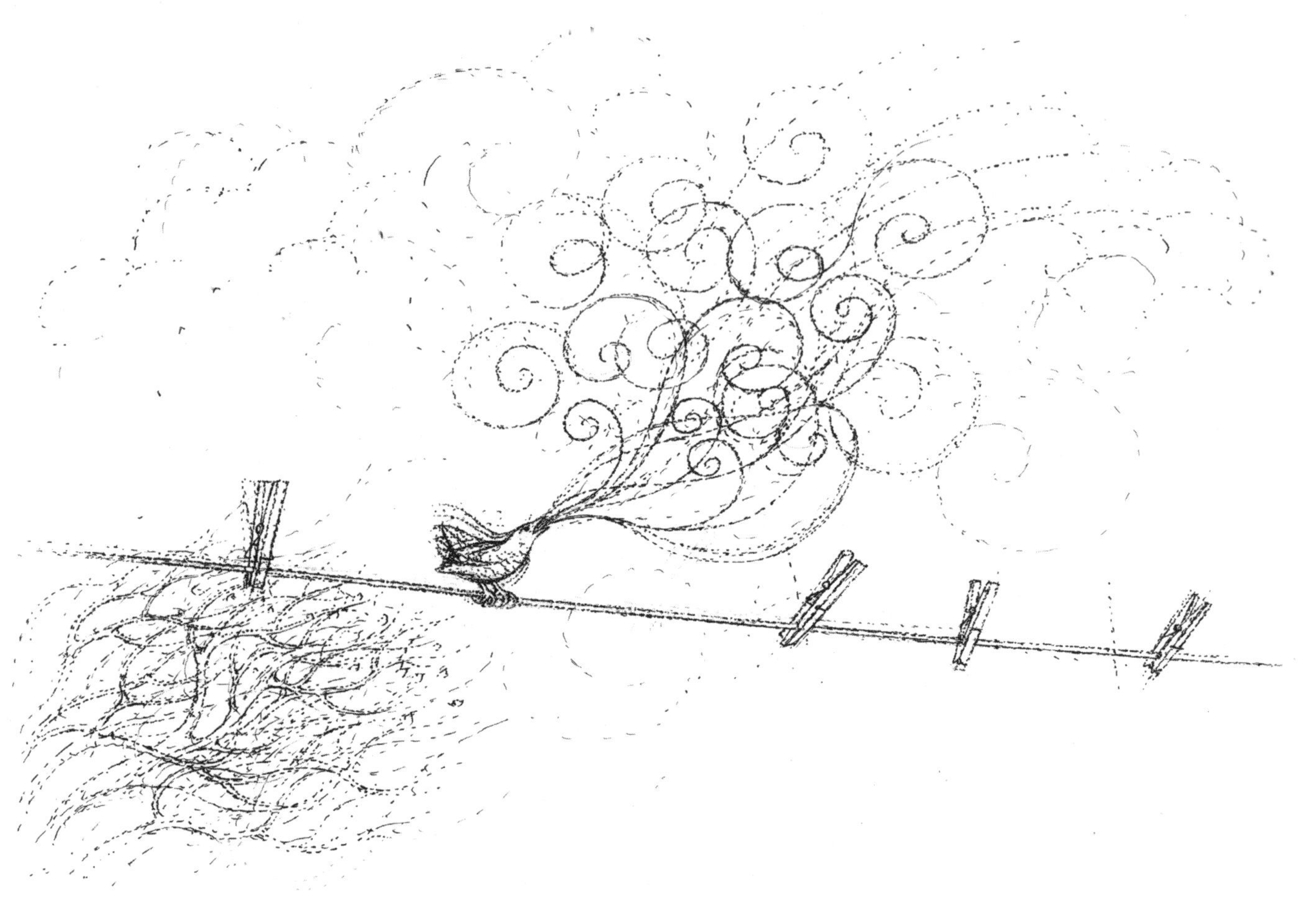

**Early morning:**
wren singing on a clothes line
(Resurgence)
indian ink
22.5 x 32 cm

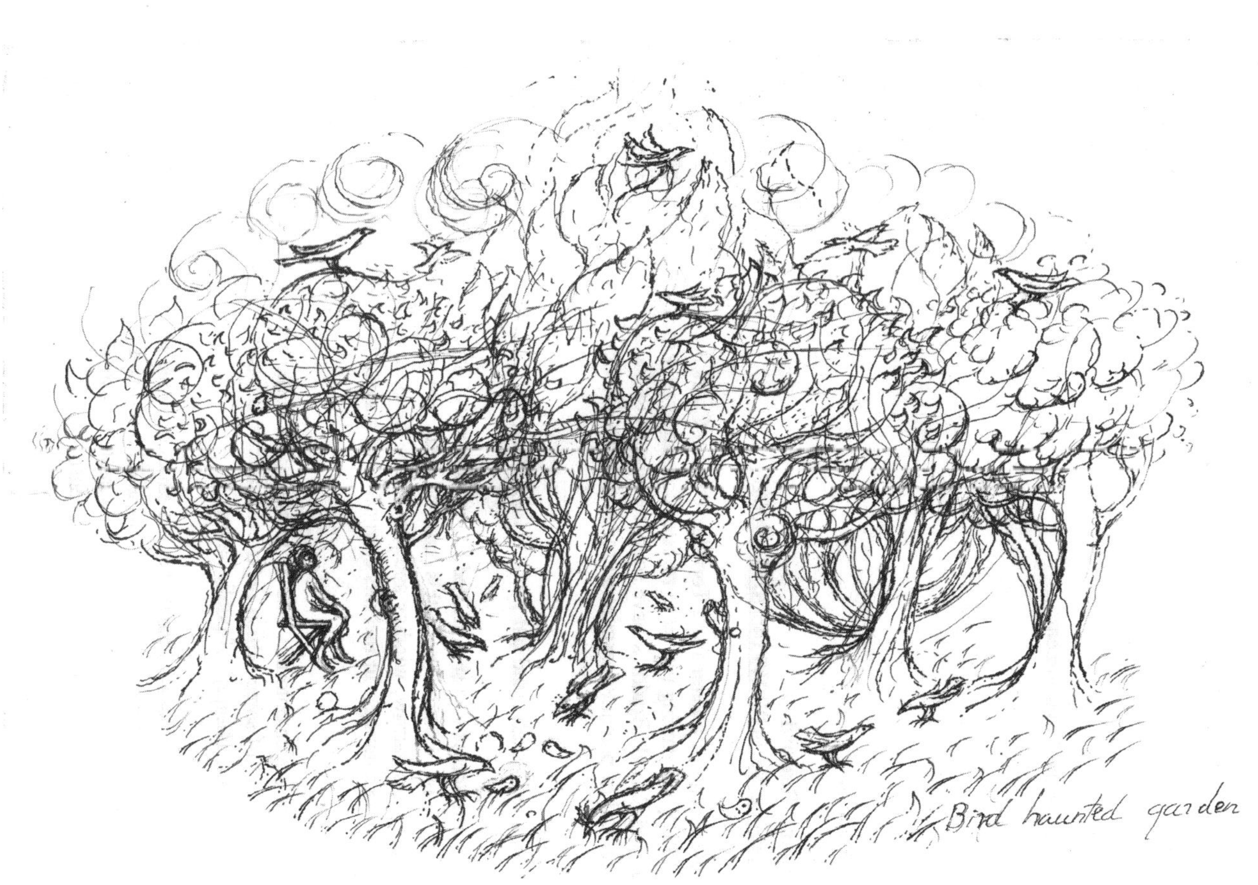


**Bird Garden**

indian ink

15 x 21 cm

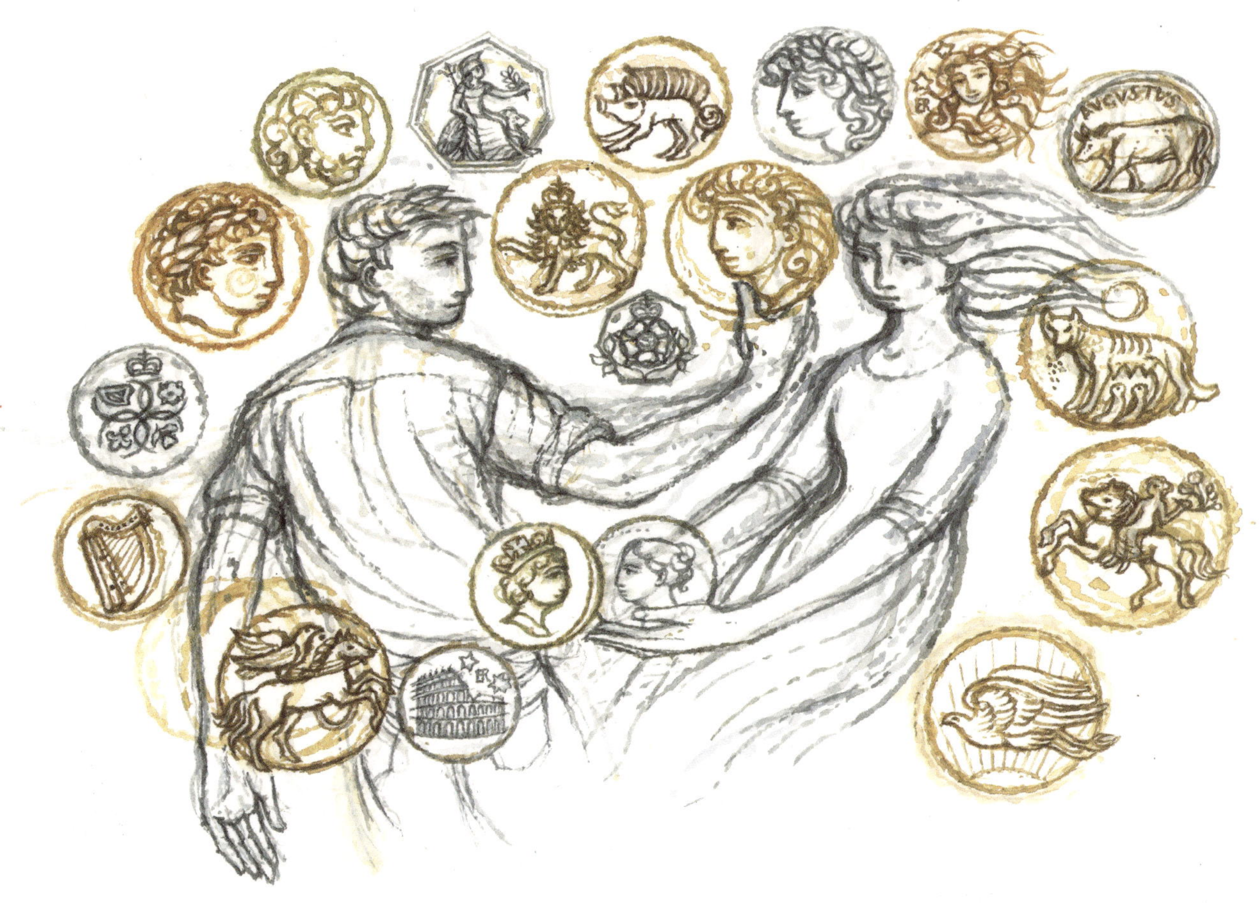


**Coins ancient and modern**
(Resurgence)
watercolour
23 x 30.5 cm

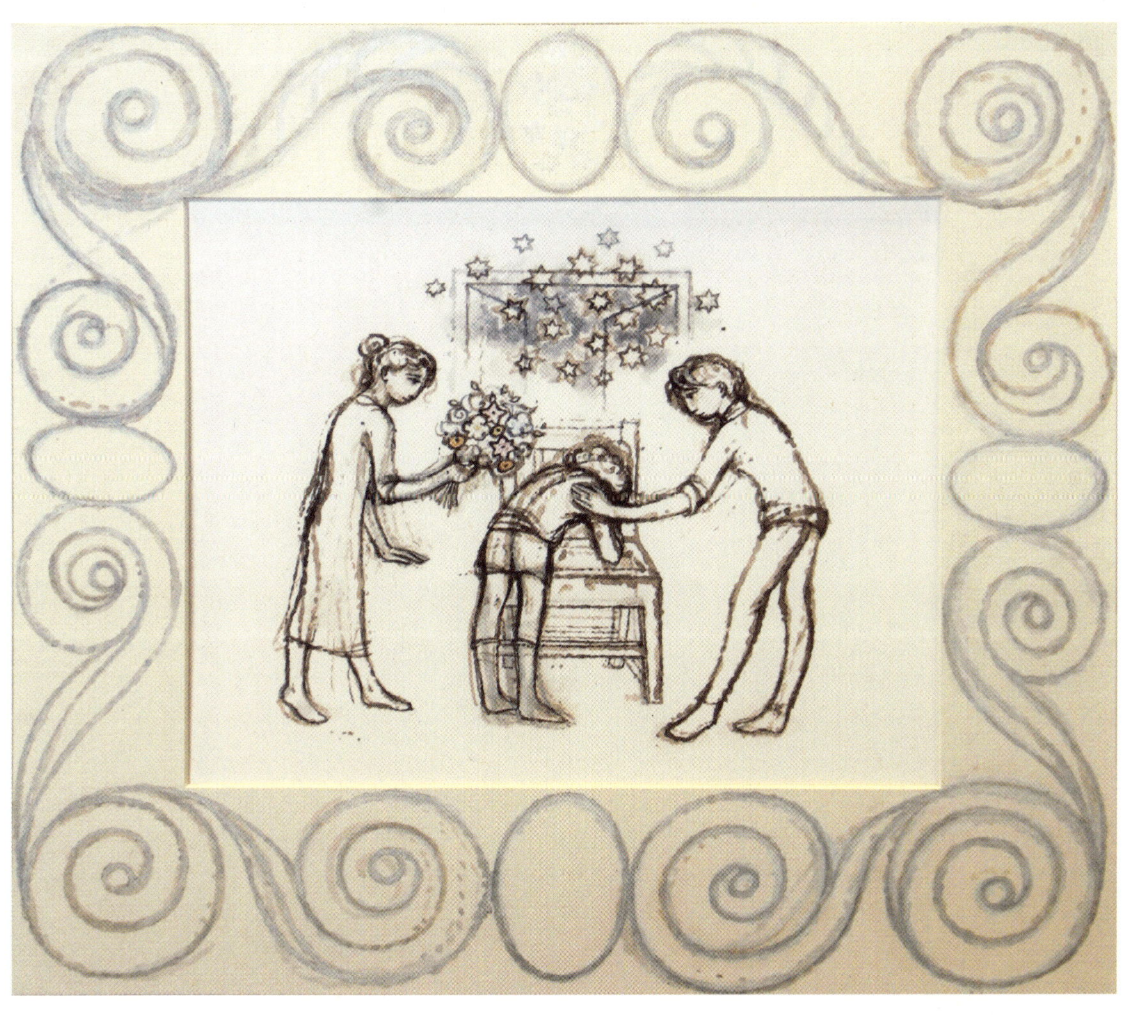

**A time for healing:**
a young boy is comforted by friends
watercolour
35 x 39.5 cm

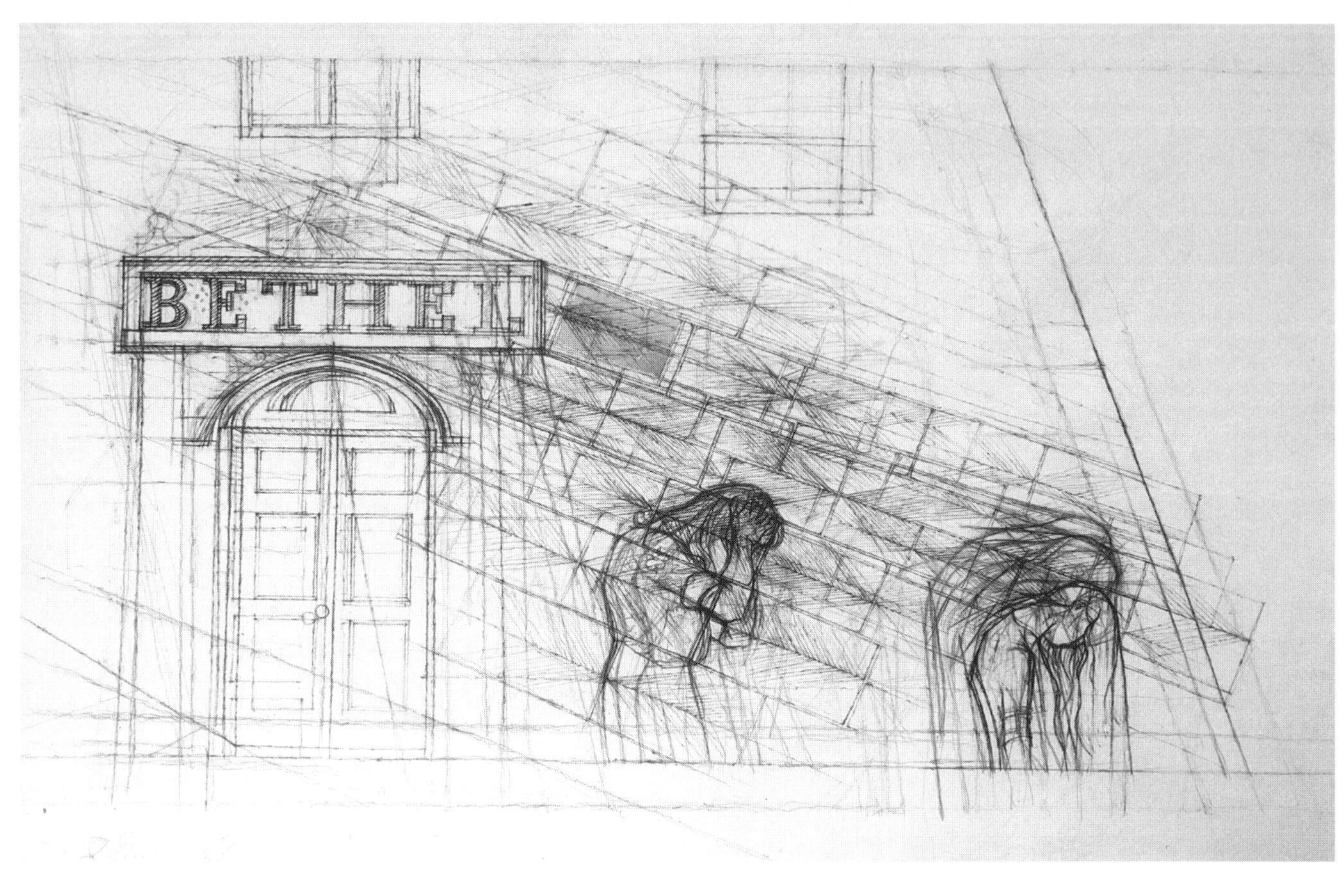


**Chapel at Staithes**
pencil
51 x 75 cm

A grim fishing village on the North Yorkshire coast. High cliffs and a dangerous harbour. The chapel is severe, powerful and impressive: a bastion against the terrible power of the sea. Through the architecture comes a sense of drama, grief and courage.

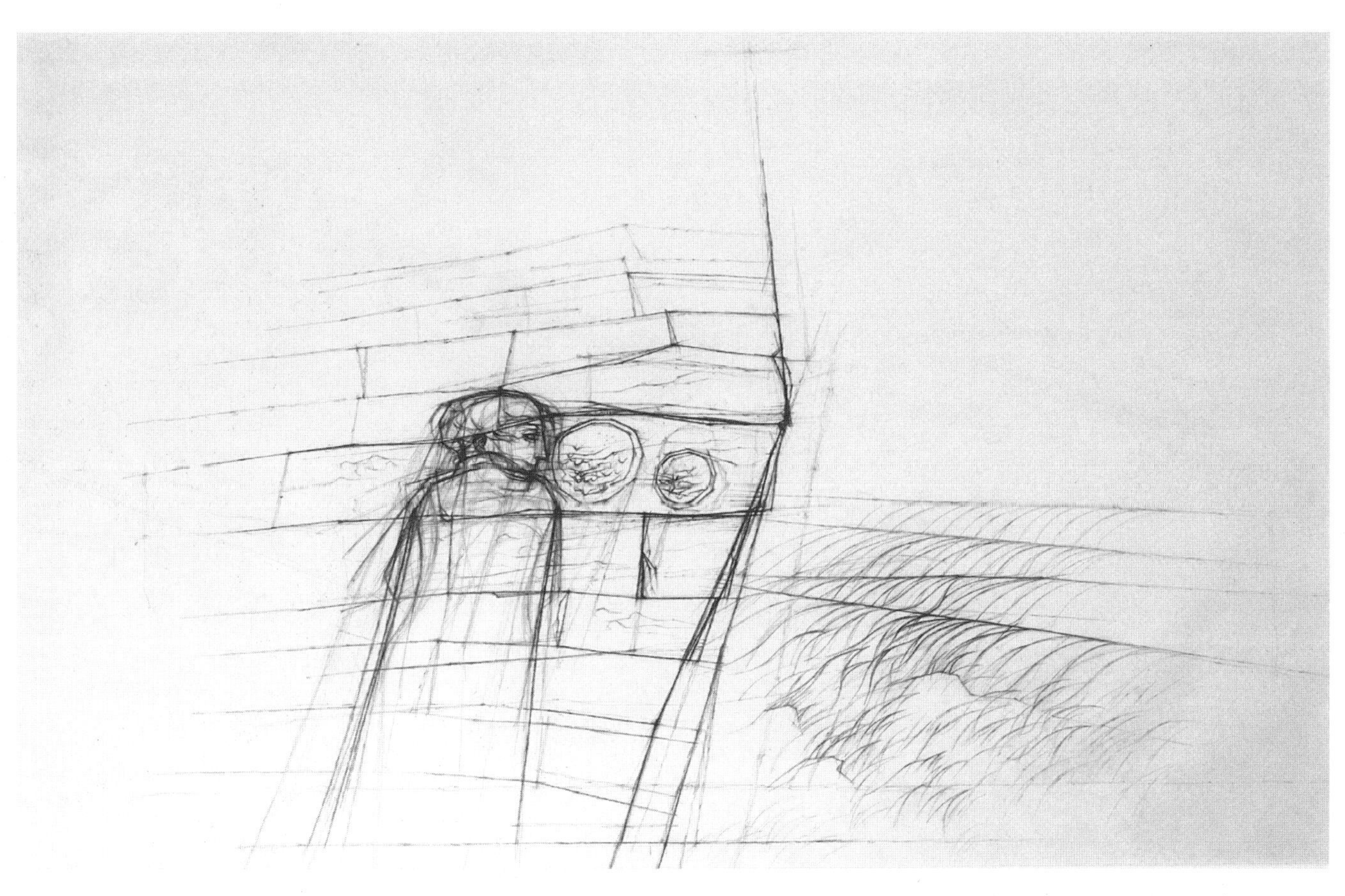

**Woman by a wall**
pencil
50.5 x 75 cm

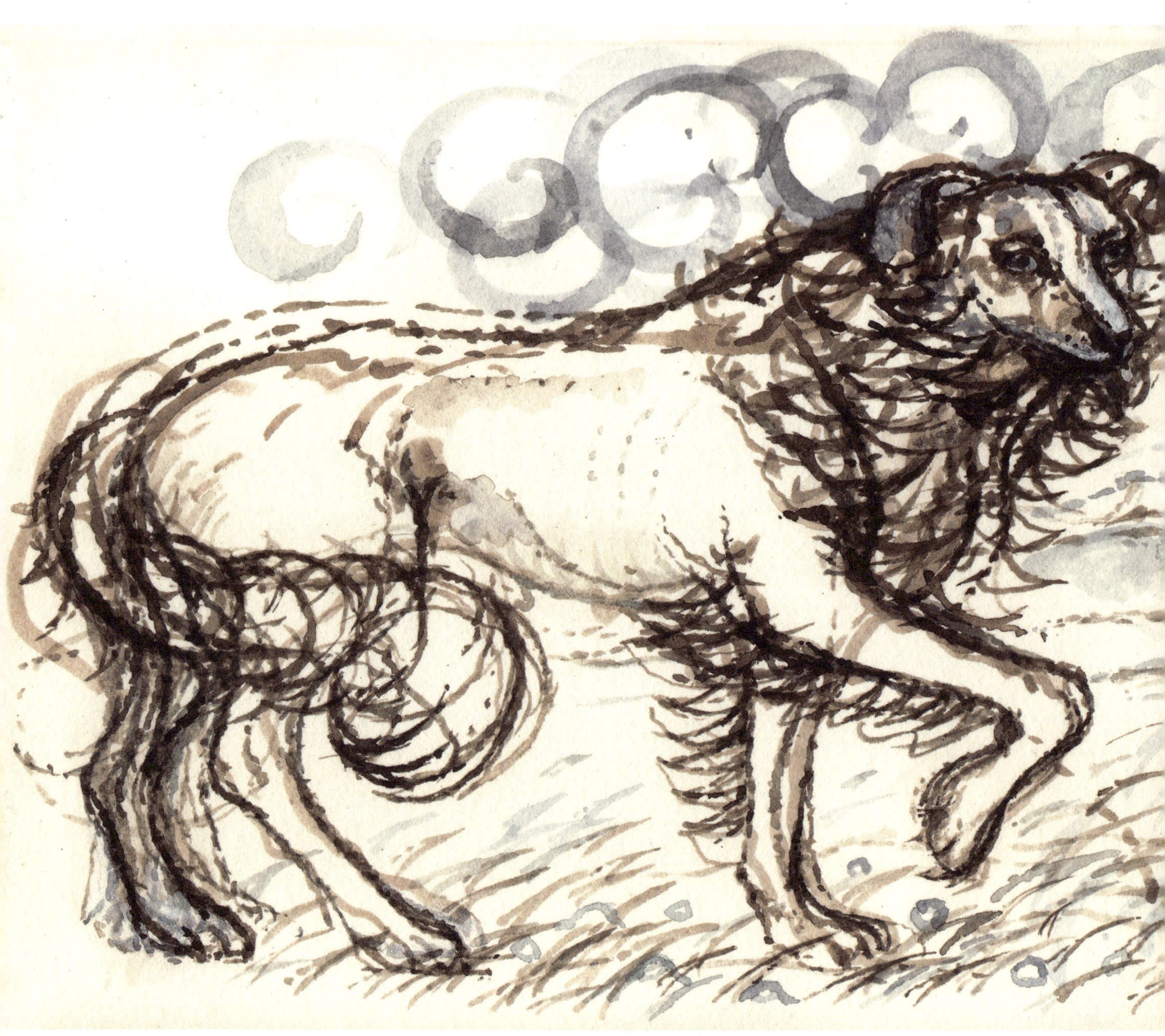

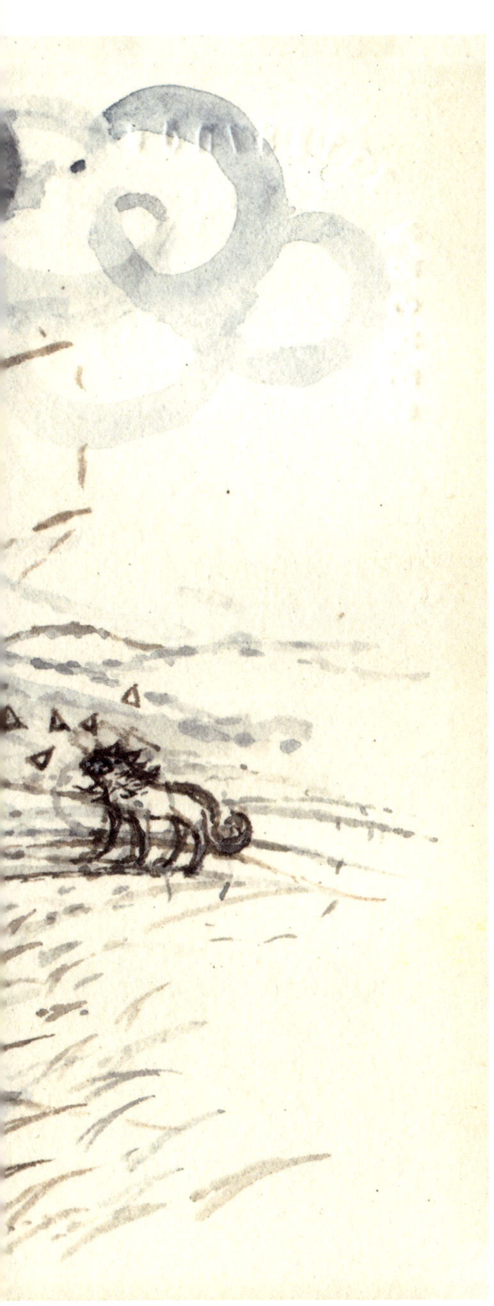

**Two dogs in the good old 18th century tradition**

watercolour

14.5 x 23 cm

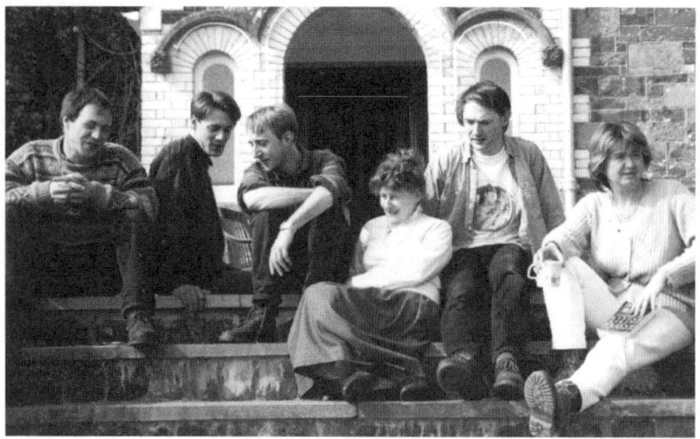

Truda and her family, turn of the century.

## TRUDA LANE (b. Harrow, 1930)

After a Convent School education, Truda Lane studied at Ealing College of Art and the Slade (where she was awarded prizes for figure & landscape drawing and a scholarship for extended study). Before teaching Art at Bury Grammar and the North London Collegiate School, Truda worked at the College of Arms in London.

In 1958 she married John, a painter and writer, whom she had met at the Slade. The couple moved to Yorkshire and lived on and near the North Yorkshire moors; between 1960 and 1969 they had four sons. After 1965 Truda and John moved to a very different kind of countryside – the alley of the River Torridge at Beaford in North Devon which has never ceased to delight. But alongside all these moves and responsibilities Truda has continued to draw whenever and wherever possible.

### Exhibitions

University of York (1968); Westward TV open exhibition, (award winner) (1973); Beaford Centre (1974); South West Arts Touring Exhibition (1974-76); "See More Art", South West Arts promotional exhibition (1976); Burton Art Gallery (1980); Dartington Arts (1982); Plough Arts Centre, Torrington (1984); Dartington Arts (with John Lane) (1984); Dartington Hall retrospective (1994).

### Commissioned work

Truda has illustrated: Learning by Heart, a book of poetry (Small School, 1986); Three Stories by John Moat (1995, Typographeum, 1995); Big World, Little World – A Green Anthology of Poetry and Prose, compiled by Sue Stewart (Thomas Nelson and Son, 1991); Only Connect, The Best of Resurgence magazine 1990-1999 (Green Books, 2000); You Are Therefore I Am (2002, Green Books); Spiritual Compass by Satish Kumar (2007, Green Books); Earth Pilgrim by Satish Kumar (2009, Green Books); Lifelines – selected drawings of Truda Lane (2010, Resurgence).

In addition, Truda's drawings have been a regular feature in the pages of the bi-monthly ecological magazine, Resurgence.

### Acknowledgement to lenders

Thank you to friends and family for their kind cooperation in lending pictures for reproduction in this book.

Published by Resurgence Trust
Ford House, Hartland, Bideford EX39 6EE UK
www.resurgence.org

Distributed by Green Books Ltd
Foxhole, Dartington, Totnes, TQ9 6EB
www.greenbooks.co.uk



ISBN 978 1 900322 95 9

Designed by Simon Willby

Printed by Kingfisher Print & Design, Totnes
Printed with eco-friendly inks on 50% recycled paper